THE CHARACTER OF PHILIP II

The Problem of Moral Judgments in History

PROBLEMS IN EUROPEAN CIVILIZATION

UNDER THE EDITORIAL DIRECTION OF
Ralph W. Greenlaw* and Dwight E. Lee†

Other volumes in preparation

9/66

PROBLEMS IN EUROPEAN CIVILIZATION

THE
CHARACTER OF PHILIP II

*The Problem of Moral Judgments
in History*

EDITED WITH AN INTRODUCTION BY

John C. Rule and John J. TePaske

THE OHIO STATE UNIVERSITY

D. C. HEATH AND COMPANY · BOSTON

Englewood   ·   Indianapolis   ·   Dallas   ·   San Francisco   ·   Atlanta

Library of Congress Catalog Card number 63–12805

COPYRIGHT © 1963 BY D. C. HEATH AND COMPANY

No part of the material covered by this copyright may be reproduced
in any form without written permission of the publisher. Printed in the
United States of America

Printed September 1966

Table of Contents

Introduction

THE sixteenth century was Spain's Golden Age. During that remarkable era Spanish fleets ranged triumphant from the Gulf of Lepanto to Manila Bay. Spanish armies under such redoubtable commanders as Don John of Austria, the Duke of Alba, and Alexander Farnése (the Duke of Parma) marched victoriously across Europe from San Quentin to the bridge of Alcántara; while *conquistadores* like Hernan Cortes and the Pizarro brothers overturned the great empires of the Aztecs and the Incas, thus establishing Spanish claims to the Western Hemisphere. In the same era, Spanish captains explored and settled the coasts of Africa and Asia until by the end of the sixteenth century, Spain controlled the greatest, most majestic empire the world had ever seen.

At the heart of this empire lay the Iberian peninsula. Here late in the fifteenth century Isabella of Castile and Ferdinand of Aragon, known as the Catholic Kings, joined to break the power of the feudal nobles and to drive the last Moorish armies from European soil. In the next generation during the reign of Charles I (Charles V of the Holy Roman Empire), grandson of Ferdinand and Isabella, Spain reached political maturity. Charles united in his person the vast Spanish, Burgundian, and Austrian possessions of the Hapsburgs and ruled at once over Spain, Burgundy, the Low Countries, most of Italy, Austria, Germany, Bohemia, and Hungary. Although harried by the Lutheran revolt in Germany and the conspiracies of the French and the Turks, Charles made the Hapsburgs the arbiters of European politics. Indeed when he abdicated the imperial throne in 1556, leaving his son Philip II on the throne of Spain and his brother Ferdinand as Holy Roman Emperor, Hapsburg hegemony on the continent of Europe seemed assured.

Philip II (1527–1598) was one of Spain's most typical yet at the same time most enigmatic kings. The eldest son of Charles V, Philip inherited Spain, Naples, the Two Sicilies, Milan, the Brabant, Flanders, the Dutch Netherlands, Franche-Comté, and the Spanish Empire in America, Africa, and Asia. From an early age his tutors had reminded him that he was the son of the greatest monarch in Europe and that he would one day inherit his father's throne. Grave, self-possessed, dignified, and responsible, Philip seemed admirably fitted for the role of European sovereign. At the age of twelve his father appointed him regent of Spain, and from that time until his death in 1598, he played a pre-eminent role in European politics. For the most part he remained deeply attached to Spain. Three years after he assumed the throne, Philip signed a peace treaty with France at Cateau-Cambrésis in 1559 and returned home to Spain, never to leave the Iberian peninsula again.

The next thirty years (1559–1588) were Philip's most productive. He consolidated his Mediterranean holdings by warring on the Moslems, first in North Africa, then in the great sea battle of Lepanto off the coast of Greece in 1571. In Italy his armies held back the French and frightened the local princelings, including the Pope, into abject submission. In Portugal, when the House of Aviz died out in 1581, Philip pressed his claims to the crown and eventually seized the country. In Spain Philip reformed the Spanish judicial system, asserted royal power in Aragon and Andalusia, enforced the royal will on ecclesiastics and local officials, and carried through extensive public works projects. Philip did, in fact, dominate Europe.

But these same years were also tragic ones. Unrest in the Low Countries turned into revolt, due in part to Philip's inflexible policies and in part to the irresponsibility and self-seeking nature of the local Flemish nobles like William of Orange. The Dutch revolt, extending from 1567 to the end of Philip's reign and after, was a constant drain on Spanish money and manpower and a vexing problem for Philip, who never could fathom the Dutch temperament. At the same time Philip quarreled with England over privateers preying upon Spanish treasure fleets and over the fate of Mary, Queen of Scots. Trouble also broke out with France over the spread of Protestantism in that kingdom and over the succession to the French throne. Although essentially a man of peace, Philip found himself continually embroiled in war. These ventures proved costly, so costly in fact that Philip repudiated his debts seven times during his reign — this despite the flow of treasure from the New World and of taxes and tribute from the Old.

Tragedy also stalked Philip's personal life. Before he had reached sixty, he had buried seventeen members of the royal family. His eldest son, Don Carlos, who was mentally unbalanced and physically retarded, became increasingly more difficult as he grew into young manhood. In early 1568 he had become so unmanageable that for his own safety and the well-being of those around him he was confined to a bare room under the guard of the Duke of Feria. By the middle of the summer Carlos was dead from undetermined causes. From this unhappy affair

arose the legend of Don Carlos, a legend which associated Philip with the murder of his son. In 1580 William the Silent repeated the tale in his *Apologia*, which was widely published and widely accepted throughout Europe.

1588 marks the watershed in Philip's reign. In that year, after months of feverish preparations, the great Spanish fleet — the Invincible Armada — sailed from Lisbon. Unable to humble Elizabethan England by indirect means, Philip had decided on a frontal assault, a crusade against the heretics of the North. With 30,000 men in 130 vessels under the command of the Duke of Medina Sidonia, Philip planned to rendezvous on the coast of Flanders with another large Spanish force and from there launch a full-scale invasion of England. This plan, however, failed disastrously. The maneuverable English fleet easily dispersed the Armada into the violent waters of the North Sea, where, buffeted by storms and lured to ruin on the inhospitable shores of Scotland and Ireland, over half the great fleet perished. With the defeat of the Armada Spanish power began a slow dignified decline; Philip, working untiringly in his small apartment in the Escorial until his painful death in 1598, never quite regained his confidence in the future. Stoically he seems to have accepted the opinion of his ambassador in Paris, who said: "It may be that God chooses to humble those who fight in His cause so that through humility they may learn the way to victory."

Philip's awesome figure has inspired a host of legends. But if we are to penetrate the mysteries that surround the man, we must first examine his inheritance. He was Castilian both by inclination and by blood. Born and reared in Spain, he represented the moral and religious fervor of his great-grandmother, Isabella, who struggled to unite Spain by means of a holy crusade against the infidel Moors. Her religious passion and her political astuteness were born again in Philip. Indeed, Philip's moral intensity, his profound piety, and his love of all things Castilian owe more, it would seem, to an inheritance from his great-grandmother than to the more direct legacy from his father, the Emperor Charles V. Charles was a man of cosmopolitan tastes and interests, an indefatigable traveler, an able linguist, an active soldier, withal a prince of the Renaissance. His son Philip was more reserved, more rigidly Spanish, outwardly more pious, a child of the Counter Reformation, who preferred the serenity and simplicity of his remote palace at the Escorial to the pomp and panoply of a lavish court. To his enemies in England and France, and even to his own subjects in Flanders and Italy, Philip became the symbol of tyranny, the upholder of religious bigotry, and the champion of Castilian supremacy. Still, despite the differences between father and son, which were often exaggerated by contemporaries, Philip carried out, in a large part, the plans originally outlined by his father. Thus, as his father would have wanted, Philip strove to keep France divided, to drive the Turks from the western Mediterranean, and to subject the Italian princes to his will. But as the years passed, the responsibilities inherited from Charles and the limitations of his own personality overwhelmed Philip. His defense against the world was to retreat from it and devote himself to the routine work of imperial administration. In time he became a kind of chief clerk upon whose judgment princes and viceroys waited — sometimes for months or even years. As one Spanish functionary observed: "If God decreed my death through the Escorial, I would be immortal."

As Philip grew older and his responsibilities more burdensome, his own conduct in a large measure fostered the myths that surrounded him. His enemies labelled him the "Devil to the South," the "weaver of plots" whose ways were mysterious, treacherous, and unscrupulous. As a recluse he came to represent the model Machiavellian, the lover of "by paths and indirect crook'd ways," or "the great father of lies who sat in the Escorial," the Catholic zealot, the "spider king." But to his Spanish subjects, he was Philip the Prudent — magnanimous, just devoted to his people and his church. To them he was the saintly, stoical successor to Saint Louis, the living symbol of the Counter Reformation, trying to steer a moderate course between the extremes of Catholic ultramontanism and cynical erastianism. Thus, like the austere grey walls of the Escorial, Philip's personality presented and still presents a forbidding façade to the world; and like the Escorial, the stern exterior hides behind it a confusing maze of character patterns that have sought explanation from that day to this.

The conflicting assessments of Philip's character bring the question of historical interpretation squarely before the student. Which of the various estimates of Philip are we to accept? Interpretations differ radically; how can they be reconciled or even explained? For the most part these are not based on contradictory evidence; they differ because of the historian's conflicting moral and ethical standards or because of his differing national biases or prejudices. Our special problem is moral judgment in history and its effect upon historical interpretation.

Historians have approached the problem of moral judgments in various ways. One tendency is toward moral relativism. The relativist eschews moral judgments altogether on the grounds that the historian, regardless of his preparation and his degree of objectivity, is subjective. His selection and arrangement of evidence, his choice of words, and his emphasis are all subject to personal whims and fancies. The moral relativist feels too that the "facts, multitudinous and beyond calculation . . . do not select themselves or force themselves automatically into a fixed scheme; instead they arrange themselves in the historian's mind as he sees them, and he sees them always through a veil of time, place, circumstance, interest, predilection, and culture." The historian thus can never reach the Rankean ideal of the "disembodied spirit," which is nothing but a noble dream. How then, argues the relativist, can the historian judge actors and events of the past and become moral arbiter for his age? He cannot even rise above the hurly-burly of contemporary morés and politics.

The moral relativist also rejects moral absolutes, at least as seen in history. He cannot accept the view that there are fixed standards of good and evil applicable to all men for all time. He feels that evil to one man may be good to another, or sin in one period may be virtue in another. Philip II, for example, can be judged as upright, God-fearing, and just by a Spanish archbishop; on the other hand, a Dutch Protestant may condemn him as a murderous, cruel bigot. At the same time, argues the relativist, even if there are moral absolutes, the historian cannot assume the Olympian position from which to render a verdict.

Still another reason given for eschewing moral judgments is that it is never clear whether to judge motives or effects. If Philip's Inquisition is judged in terms of effects, for example, it becomes an instrument of religious persecution perpetrated by a misguided zealot. If, however, it is judged in terms of motives, the Inquisition stands as a Christian institution, an agency of high-minded, devout men for the elimination of heresy and the strengthening of the one true church. From the standpoint of effects Philip II's character may be described as cruel, sadistic, treacherous, and murderous; yet from the standpoint of his motives he may be justified as a devout Catholic and loyal Spaniard, working in union with God to serve the interest of the church and the state. With this difficulty in mind, the relativist ideally hopes to avoid judgments based either on motives or on effects.

This same school of historiography also questions the ultimate value of moral judgments. Moral condemnation, it is argued, will provide no useful lesson for mankind except to prove, as Herbert Butterfield has pointed out, that all men are to a greater or lesser degree sinners. At the same time making moral judgments may actually be a disservice to society, for they may prove that immorality, political immorality in particular, often pays, that treachery, deceit, and murder may be absolutely essential for political success.

At the other end of the spectrum from the relativists are those historians who stress the need for moral commitment in a world filled with the chaos of shattered ideals. These historians believe with Lord Acton that they must "suffer no man and no cause to escape the undying penalty which history has the power to inflict on wrong." Those urging moral commitment assume that there are absolute standards from which to make moral judgments, and that the historian is qualified to act as supreme arbiter. Good and evil are universal qualities, applicable to all societies for all periods in history. Mercy and murder may be praised or condemned on the same basis whether in the first, sixth, twelfth, or twentieth century. There is, however, some disagreement in how to apply these moral absolutes. Some argue the necessity of condemning both the individual and his deeds. Others believe it possible to separate the individual from his evil acts. In other words it is possible to explain or understand individual immorality historically while at the same time condemning the deed itself. Thus historians may say that Philip II perpetrated the worst of human crimes, but they may be justified as the acts of God's personal agent and the king of Spain acting against Protestant heresy and threats to the Spanish state. This does not mean, they assert, that the auto-de-fé, judicial torture, murder, and cruelty may be excused. They were evil both by sixteenth-century standards and our own.

Still another argument on the side of this school of history goes something like this. The historian will inevitably make moral judgments; he cannot help himself. But it is his prerogative if not his duty to do so. As a moral man his reader will assume a moral stance, even toward the most impersonal presentation. With a deeper understanding of the forces and individuals at work in the period under investigation, the historian has the obligation to pass his own judgments. Going beyond mere explanation and description, he can thus make his craft a nobler, higher calling.

No figure in modern history brings this problem of moral judgments more sharply into focus than Philip II. He is in fact a classic example. No individual has aroused more bitter disputes over character, motives, and policy than this Spanish king who dominated Europe for half a century. On the one side he has been accused of the most horrible of crimes — cruelty, treachery, adultery, incest, witchcraft, murder, and a host of other offenses. For many, he has become the incarnation of all that is evil in man. Equally potent on the other side are the views of his proponents, who picture Philip as wise, just, prudent, benevolent, hard-working, a devoted father and husband, pious Christian, and patron of the arts. Standing somewhere between these two extremes are those who seek neither to vindicate nor to condemn Philip, but to understand and explain Philip's actions within the limits of his time, his personality, and the forces at work during his reign. Samples of all three views are included in this volume.

Among the diatribes most damaging to Philip's character was the *Apologia* of William the Silent. As the spokesman for Dutch independence and for a vigorous Protestant minority, William pictures Philip as the villainous symbol of evil and oppression, the living representation of the degeneracy and moral decadence of the Spanish people. Written in reply to Philip's proscription of 1580, the *Apologia* accused the Spanish king of murder, incest, and inhuman cruelty. For William these charges masked deeper political and personal motives, but they served as an effective instrument for undermining Spanish rule in the Netherlands. Widely circulated throughout the continent, the *Apologia* was a convenient document for discrediting Philip and the Spanish people.

The publication of the *Apologia* provided an important stimulus for the growth of the Black Legend. This Legend portrayed Philip and the Spanish people as evil, barbarous, obscurantist tyrants, who were morally unfit to rule over their vast dominions. This view was supported by the stories of Bartolomé de las Casas, a Dominican friar who recounted Spanish atrocities in the New World, and by the *Relaciones* (1594) of Antonio Pérez, erstwhile minister of Philip II who had fallen out of royal favor in the late 1570's. These sources gave England, France, and Holland the moral justification for attacking the Spanish Empire. Putting their struggle against Spain in terms of good and evil, they found a convenient rationalization and justification for carving out their own empires in both Europe and America.

During the eighteenth century, Philip's detractors continued their attacks, but for different reasons. After Philip's death the power of Spain had declined. In the seventeenth and eighteenth centuries, first France and then Great Britain dominated Europe. Nationalism and imperialism thus became less important as the motives for condemning Philip. But the currents of thought fostered by the Scientific Revolution and the Enlightenment brought a new spirit to Europe. To this new age the character of Philip II was completely alien. He was, in fact, the antithesis of the Enlightenment. His strict religious orthodoxy became bigotry to men preaching tolerance and understanding. As an absolute monarch directing a highly centralized administrative system, he was completely out of tune with the eighteenth-century doctrines of popular sovereignty, social contract, and general will. Philip II was, in fact, the historical model of all that the Enlightenment philosophers railed against — bigotry, intolerance, inhumanity, oppression, injustice, and despotism. Robert Watson's late eighteenth-century view of Philip was influ-

enced, at least in part, by the Enlightenment and was well received by those
caught up in the ideals of the Age of
Reason. Watson condemned Philip's "sanguinary spirit," his "bigoted zeal," and "unrelenting cruelty." But Watson was not
completely a product of Enlightenment
Europe. He was also influenced by his
Protestant theological training, which
added a special warmth to his acrimonious
attacks on Philip.

In the nineteenth and twentieth centuries Philip's most bitter critics were stern
Protestant moralists like John Lothrop
Motley and Cecil John Cadoux. They
viewed Philip in terms of their Protestantism, their belief in moral absolutes, and
Enlightenment ideals. Both men judged
him in terms of effects, not motives. Motley
finds Philip to be one of the most repre-
hensible figures in human history, guilty
of the worst offenses against mankind and
God. "The horrible monotony of his career," says Motley, "stupifies the mind
until it is ready to accept the principle of
evil as the fundamental law of the world."
More subtle and sophisticated, Cadoux is
willing to recognize the limits placed on
Philip's actions and policies. However, Cadoux stands firmly on his belief in moral
absolutes and condemns Philip II from this
standpoint.

Sir Charles Oman's bitter attack on
Philip II is more difficult to assess. Historically Oman understands Philip's reign,
but he has taken an intense personal dislike to the Prudent King which both colors
and enlivens his narrative. Forsaking the
standards upon which he assesses other historical figures, such as Charles V, he condemns Philip more on personal than on
moral grounds and holds defects in Philip's
character responsible for all failures in
Spanish policy. Oman, it appears, belongs
to that school which believes that value
judgments add verve to the narrative and
that it is incumbent upon the historian
to make such assessments. His view of
Philip II is typical of the kind of reaction

the Prudent King may set off among historians.

Philip's defenders are no less numerous.
Well-beloved in his own country, he is
still looked upon as one of the greatest
Spanish kings, ruler of Spain in its Golden
Age. His contemporaries or near contemporaries in the Iberian peninsula, Luis
Cabrera de Córdoba and Ferdinand de los
Cobos, have perpetuated the image of a
virtuous, wise, moderate, and just monarch.
Through Spanish Catholic eyes he was
seen as a sincere patriot and devout defender of the church, truly the Spanish
successor to Saint Louis. For the most part
these views of Philip continued in Spain
until the twentieth century when more
dispassionate historians began to assess his
reign.

Modern-day apologists for Philip II like
Antonio Ballesteros y Beretta and W. H.
Walsh based their defense of the king
more on history than on patriotism. Com-
paring Philip with his contemporaries
Elizabeth of England and Catherine de
Medici of France, both Ballesteros and
Walsh find Philip moderate and wise in
his handling of almost unsurmountable
national and imperial problems. For them
his methods and policies set a high standard of morality and may be contrasted
favorably with those of his counterparts
in England and France. These modern-
day defenders of Philip also see the best
in him personally, sometimes in the face
of strong evidence to the contrary.

Philip was not rescued from the polemi-
cists (on either side) until the early nineteenth century. The historian most responsible for rehabilitating the Spanish
monarch was Leopold von Ranke (1795–
1886), who was the most famous member
of the new school of scientific historians
emerging in the early 1800's. By scientific
history Ranke and his contemporaries
meant an impartial, detached view of the
past as distinct from the highly romanti-
cized or vigorously partisan histories often
presented by the panegyrists and pam-
phleteers of the seventeenth and eighteenth

centuries. What made Ranke famous among members of the historical guild was his use of documents. Seldom had an historian before his time so immersed himself in the historical past. Ranke visited local German archives and libraries and travelled in Italy, France, and England, ransacking archival records there. He uprooted vast numbers of diplomatic dispatches, diaries, journals, council minutes, memoranda, and the like; and his work stimulated a renaissance in historical study. It was through his vast knowledge of the sources — particularly his close reading of the Venetian ambassadors' *relazioni* or reports from Spain — that Ranke was able to portray Philip as a human being, neither devil nor saint, but rather as a timid man, wholly devoted to his family, a man who shouldered the burden of running the state because, like Louis XIV and Frederick the Great after him, he felt it was the task to which God had appointed him.

Still, Ranke's balanced presentation of Philip had few emulators in the nineteenth century. The works of Macaulay, Prescott, and Motley, with their predominantly Anglo-Saxon, Whig, Protestant bias, drove the works of more sober historians like Ranke off the popular bookshelf. For the most part, the view of Philip as a Catholic bigot, bent upon conquering Europe for the greater glory of God and Empire, remained popular. Still, Ranke made his mark and recruited followers. One of them, the Belgian archivist and historian, Louis Prosper Gachard, diligently collected Philip's correspondence, re-examined the established view of the Spanish monarch on such things as the Don Carlos legend, and suggested many new paths of investigation for the student of Philippine Spain to follow. His many collections of documents and his careful research, in the Rankean tradition, did much to challenge the traditional picture of Philip II.

Near the end of the nineteenth century, the Danish historian Carl Georg Bratli carried the reassessment of Philip's character even further when he reprinted vari-

ous letters of Philip that he had come upon in the Spanish archives at Simancas. From Bratli's investigations Philip emerges as a human if not humane ruler; a patient, painstaking administrator; a patron of the arts; but a man of mediocre ability pricked by a passionate sense of duty. Bratli's comparatively well-balanced treatment opened wide the floodgates of revisionism and rehabilitation.

In America Roger B. Merriman, following Bratli's lead, did a great deal to put Philip in a broader historical perspective. Merriman labored over contemporary accounts of Philip and traveled to European archives, particularly those in Spain, where he unearthed more Spanish state papers, memoranda of council meetings, and personal letters of Philip's family and intimates. Though not brilliant, his portrait of Philip is judiciously wrought, meticulously balanced, and scrupulously fair. He incorporated almost a hundred years of new scholarship from Ranke's time to his own and quite consciously counters the Whig interpretation of Philip, which presented him as the evil master of the Armada, the hated tyrant, the secretive plotter, and the archenemy of Elizabeth I and of all things good and decent.

Merriman's work was carried on by his student Garrett Mattingly, who like his mentor, carried on research in many European archives. From Mattingly's extensive investigations comes one of the most lifelike portrayals of Philip and his court and a deep sympathy for the period of the sixteenth century. In both *Renaissance Diplomacy* (1955) and *The Armada* (1959), the reader senses the humanness of the setting — the careless errors committed by diplomats and prelates; the accidents attendant on the launching of the Armada; the confusion, pettiness, selfishness, and spite shown by the actors in the drama. Yet their shortsightedness and stupidities are cleverly juxtaposed with their occasional glimpses of the future and their desire to do good. Out of the sixteenth century Mattingly creates an era with which we can sympathize and for which we can obtain a measure of understanding. Certainly his portrait of Philip is at once sympathetic and realistic. In Mattingly as in Davies, Bertrand, Bratli, Altamira, and Ranke, we see the well-meaning statesman, plagued by ill health and bad luck; the patient clerk overwhelmed by the cares of his office; the dutiful man who was neither sanguinary nor sanguine. Such is the man who has emerged from the moderate school of historians. What is your judgment?

CHRONOLOGICAL TABLE

1527   Birth of Philip.

1543   Philip's marriage to Princess María Manuela of Portugal. Philip becomes Regent of Spain.

1545   Death of María after the birth of one son, Carlos.

1548–1550   Philip travels to Italy, Germany, and the Low Countries.

1554   Philip's marriage to Mary Tudor of England. Philip receives the title King of Naples.

1556   Abdication of Charles I. Philip becomes Philip II of Spain.

1558   Death of Mary Tudor. Death of Charles I. Elizabeth Tudor becomes Queen of England. The Battle of Gravelines.

1559   Treaty of Cateau Cambrésis. Philip weds Elizabeth of Valois.

1563   Philip begins construction of the Escorial.

1565   The Compromise of Breda. Beginnings of the Dutch Revolt.

1567   The Duke of Alba, governor of the Low Countries, institutes harsh policies.

1568   Death of Elizabeth of Valois, who bore Philip two children, Isabel Clara Eugenia and Catalina Micaela. Death of Prince Don Carlos.

1571   Spanish naval victory at Lepanto.

1572   Massacre of the Huguenots in Paris on the Eve of Saint Bartholomew's Day.

1573   The Duke of Resquens replaces the Duke of Alba in the Low Countries.

1576   Death of the Duke of Resquens. The "Spanish Fury." Don Juan, hero of Lepanto, becomes governor of the Low Countries.

1578   Death of Don Juan and his replacement by Alexander Farnése, Duke of Parma. Rift between Philip II and Antonio Pérez.

1580   Incorporation of Portugal into the Spanish Empire. The *Apologia* of William of Orange, condemning Philip II and justifying the Dutch Revolt.

1584   Death of William of Orange. Completion of the Escorial.

1586   English alliance with the United Provinces of the Netherlands.

1588   Defeat of the Invincible Armada.

1589–91   Revolt in Aragon against Philip II.

1595   War between France and Spain.

1598   Cession of the Low Countries to Philip's daughter, Isabel Clara Eugenia. Death of Philip II. Peace of Vervins.

Conflict of Opinion

"He is, sir, devoted to virtue and justice, scorning all that is contrary to them. Wherefore we all accept and respect his advice, because in the midst of the gravity and restraint with which he gives it and points out the errors, it is accompanied by a natural majesty and authority which is terrifying."

— FRANCISCO DE LOS COBOS Y MOLINA

"Does this king deserve the title which he assumes, a minister of God, who thus confounds the distinction between vice and virtue; and thus publicly avows his willingness to bestow the highest rewards and honours upon men defiled with the most abominable crimes?"

— WILLIAM THE SILENT

"Philip began to rule Spain with justice and divine zeal far superior to his years, proving that virtue is born in kings. He spoke solemnly, responded quickly and keenly; he perceived easily and observed closely. He was cautious in dealing with complex and difficult problems; wise and thorough in all his actions, he acted always as if his personal fortune were at stake."

— LUIS CABRERA DE CÓRDOBA

"It might be expected that, in a virtuous prince, the sentiments of honour and humanity would, on some occasions, triumph over the dictates of superstition; but of this triumph, there occurs not a single instance in the reign of Philip; who, without hesitation, violates his most sacred obligations as often as religion afforded him a pretence; and under that pretence exercised for many years the most unrelenting cruelty, without reluctance or remorse."

— ROBERT WATSON

"If, on the one hand, his reserve and his gravity unfitted him for presiding over the nations he ruled with kindness, affability, and as a father; on the other hand his narrow and fanatical constitution of mind placed it far beyond his power to become the reconciling spirit of his distracted times; he was, on the contrary, a great promoter and augmenter of the discord."

— LEOPOLD VON RANKE

"If Philip possessed a single virtue it has eluded the conscientious research of the writer of these pages. If there are vices — as possibly there are — from which he was exempt, it is because it is not permitted to human nature to attain perfection even in evil."

— JOHN LOTHROP MOTLEY

"He prided himself upon his kindliness and decency, and it is quite certain that in doing so he believed himself to be sincere. He did not like fuss, disturbance, disorder, bloodshed, and execution."

— LOUIS BERTRAND

"If Philip had been merely an honest fanatic, ready to wade through any amount of blood, and to kindle any amount of fires for heretics, he would have been much less hateful than was actually the case. But he was also a systematic liar and hypocrite, who thought no means too base to secure his two great ideals — autocratic power for himself, triumph for the Roman Church."

— SIR CHARLES OMAN

"Kindness to the poor, an untiring interest in the welfare of his own servants — especially those of the humblest kind — and a zeal for social justice show themselves continually among all the strenuous labours of his long reign."

— REGINALD TREVOR DAVIES

"From first to last he was the 'Prudent King.' "

— ROGER BIGELOW MERRIMAN

"What seems to be peculiar about Philip, and is moreover completely consistent with the ethical tone which normally characterized his political behaviour, is that he seems to have imposed on himself very little moral check in the use of this unlovely instrument of kingcraft. . . . I do not see how, with the facts before us, we can do other than describe him as a cruel and intolerant bigot."

— CECIL JOHN CADOUX

"Philip II incarnated and represented the Catholic spirit of the Spanish people, and the defense of Catholicism became the most important reason for his actions. . . . Philip II acted always as a Spaniard; with dignity. His deeds were impregnated with an *hidalgo* ethic that had honor as its basis, the precious knightly legacy of the Middle Ages, which has been and is the theme of Spanish history."

— ANTONIO BALLESTEROS Y BERETTA

"There was true asceticism in the way he toiled, eyes red-rimmed, bones aching, fingers stiff, at his self-imposed task of chief clerk of the Spanish empire. Increasingly as he grew older, he gave up for it not only the hunting, dancing, and feasting which were the conventional diversions of kings, but the things he really loved, flowers and pictures, country excursions and the company of his children."

— GARRETT MATTINGLY

THE CHARACTER OF PHILIP II:
THREE SIXTEENTH-CENTURY VIEWS

Philip II as a Youth

FRANCISCO DE LOS COBOS Y MOLINA

Francisco de los Cobos y Molina (1477?–1547) spent most of his life in the service of Charles V, Philip II's father. Rising in the ranks from a menial copier of documents to the prestigious post of king's secretary, Cobos became a confidant of the Emperor and accompanied him in his travels in Germany, Italy, and the Barbary Coast. His reports provided Charles V with a wealth of information on the affairs of his Empire, and for his loyal service Charles accorded Cobos honor, riches, and a host of titles. The short selection below is taken from a report sent to Charles V when Philip was sixteen or seventeen. In 1540, at age twelve, Philip had become regent of Spain, and by the time he was fifteen he had assumed further administrative duties in the Council of Castile. As might be expected from a faithful secretary trying to ingratiate himself with his king, the report pictured Philip in glowing terms that certainly must have pleased his father. The translation is taken from Professor Hayward Keniston's thorough biography of Cobos, *Francisco de los Cobos, Secretary of the Emperor, Charles V.*

FIRST of all, sir, King Philip my lord is already so great a king that his knowledge and capacity have outstripped his years, for he seems to have achieved the impossible by his great understanding and his lofty comprehension. His diversions are a complete and constant devotion to work and the affairs of his kingdom. He is always thinking and talking about matters of good government and justice, without leaving room for favoritism or idleness or flattery or any vice. His relations and conversations are always about these matters with mature men of the highest reputation. At times he asks questions about matters in which he is informed, and this is no doubt his greatest quality, for he does it so as not to err in his commands.

In the most important affairs, where it is necessary to hold meetings to discuss them, he listens to the opinions of each one with the greatest gravity and attention; after he has heard and understood them all, with every consideration and judgment he disapproves of what does not seem good, rarely making a mistake, and afterwards he reaches his own decision, taking the best from each one, which is a source of wonder to all. And so in all this, he is doing astonishing and admirable things.

He frequently is closeted with me for hours at a time to discuss important matters of state. Afterwards he does the same thing with the President of the Council [Valdés], to study the problems of justice, and with the Duque de Alba to talk about questions of war, and with other people to talk over other very different questions, to inform

From Hayward Keniston, *Francisco de los Cobos, Secretary of the Emperor, Charles V* (Pittsburgh, n.d.), pp. 269–270. Reprinted by permission of the University of Pittsburgh Press.

1

himself in detail about his distant dominions. And afterwards he has me write out his orders and decisions in each one of these things, which he dictates to me. And although I have express instructions from Your Majesty — and he knows it — to reprove him and to advise actions more likely to achieve good, I assure Your Majesty I not only do not have to reject anything that he decides, but I am astonished at his prudent, well-considered recommendations, which are more fitting in a man trained all his life in state and other affairs than in a ruler who is so new in it, in years and in authority.

He is, sir, devoted to virtue and justice, scorning all that is contrary to them. Wherefore we all accept and respect his advice, because in the midst of the gravity and restraint with which he gives it and points out the errors, it is accompanied by a natural majesty and authority which is terrifying. Your Majesty may be sure that the King my lord was born only to be a great king.

Your Majesty is familiar with the qualities and spirit of the Duque de Alba. In spite of that, it happened one day last month that His Highness asked the Duke something about the war with France. The Duke, with his accustomed impetuosity, replied that as long as the Emperor and he were alive, they would soon take care of France. The King my lord, very quietly but with all his majesty, said to him: "After the Emperor, no one holds a place before me. I am of the opinion that anyone who does not understand that and boasts in my presence either does not know me or is trying to displease me. This should let you know who I am." With that His Highness turned his back and the rest of us who were there were amazed at his angry reply. We all had to intervene to restore the Duke to his favor.

In one hand he holds punishment for the guilty, and in the other, reward for the deserving. He rules his kingdoms with such prudence and justice that nothing is hidden from him, and he is familiar with everything. At public audiences he is so quiet and humane that by his gentleness and affability he encourages those who come with pleas. He listens attentively to everyone, which is most praiseworthy. For some he makes suitable provision; others he sends to the proper official; those who make improper requests he dismisses sternly and majestically.

He is watchful for the honor of God and the welfare of these his kingdoms. He requires that in the courts only right and justice shall prevail. He demands that offices in them shall be given only to those who are competent to fill them and he tries in every way to find whether this is being done. Finally, sir, the King my lord is acting and thinking at so high and just a level that without the aid of anyone he is capable of maintaining his kingdoms in great glory and fame and of winning for himself the name of a great king.

Youth and Early Training of Philip II:
A Late Sixteenth-Century View

LUIS CABRERA DE CÓRDOBA

No collection of essays on Philip II would be complete without a selection from Luis Cabrera de Córdoba (1559–1623). His four-volume work is a basic source for the reign of the Prudent King and contains many details about Philip unavailable elsewhere. Entering the king's employ as a youth, Cabrera served in Italy, in wars against the Turks and Venetians, and in laying plans for the Invincible Armada. While carrying out these duties, Cabrera took copious notes on Philip's reign in preparation for a biography. Something of a plagiarist, he also copied down what contemporary chroniclers, like Antonio Herrera de Torde-sillas wrote about the Spanish monarch. The first portion of Cabrera's biography on the early life of the king appeared in 1619, but the entire work was not finally published until 1876, almost 250 years later. Written in an obscure, Gongoristic style, Cabrera's work nevertheless remains as one of the richest sources of information on Philip II.

HE (Philip II) was born in Valladolid on May 21, 1527, date of the festival of Saint Segundo, martyr of Córdoba, during the pontificate of Clement VII in the Empire of his father Charles V, the great, much to the joy, hope, and gladness of his subjects. He was baptized in the monastery of Saint Paul at the Institute of Saint Dominic de Guzmán by Don Alonso de Fonseca, who, as advocate, named him after Saint Philip the apostle and in memory of his grandfather King Philip I. The Emperor did not celebrate the baptism of his first son with the expected solemnity, for, even though the matter did not ruffle his lofty exterior, he was, nevertheless, disturbed over the news concerning his army. On May 6 (without the knowledge of his Caesarean Majesty and against the wishes of his officers and viceroys in Italy), it had sacked Rome. Insolent from the memory of its victories, heady from the booty taken from unfriendly nations near the papal states, and seeking plunder and booty as a reward for its actions, the army unrestrain-edly abused its great power. It was a curious irony that vain wits considered the event as a bad omen and seriously speculated that Philip II would ruin the church; for it was his piety, obedience, wealth, shield, and sword that demonstrated how easily human judgment can be deceived. On Sunday, April 19, 1528, ten months and twenty days after his birth in the presence of his parents, the kingdoms of Spain swore allegiance to him in the monastery of Saint Jerome in Madrid. He showed special abilities so early that the Emperor began his son's education at age seven, choosing as his teacher Doctor Juan Martínez Siliceo, theologian at the University of Álcala and professor at the University of Salamanca. He (Martínez) taught Philip to love and to fear God, to read, to write, to do arithmetic — his best subject — and through interpreters to know Latin, Italian, and French. He used these languages infrequently, even though he understood them, for he hoped, like the Greeks and the Romans whose empires were not so vast,

From Luis Cabrera de Córdoba, *Felipe Segundo, Rey de España,* 4 vols. (Madrid, 1876), I, pp. 3–6. [Editors' translation.]

to make Castilian the common language throughout the world. The successes of the conquistador would help to extend use of the language in the same manner as the Greeks in Asia and the Romans and Arabs in Asia, Europe, and Africa. Philip's sanguine temperament and his deliberate melancholy manner kept him from acting on impulse and brought him (as it happened) long life, commanding appearance, sharp wit, retentive memory, a sense of justice, sincerity, grandeur, a natural sense of virtue, optimism, and a sense of humor, a quality that brought joy to many in the course of his life. Don Juan de Zúñiga, knight commander of Castile and a member of the Council of State, the tutor who schooled him in royal protocol, had little difficulty teaching Philip to act gallantly and elegantly with proper grace and courtesy. He (Philip II) guarded his dignity as royal prince closely. Once while he was still dressing, Philip was visited by Cardinal Tabera, Archbishop of Toledo, who removed his hat when he came into the presence of the prince. Zúñiga immediately gave orders to Philip that the Cardinal should be told to don his hat, (for Spanish grandees had the privilege of wearing their hats in the king's presence). Philip, however, was careful to observe the proper amenities. He first put on his own cape and hat and then said: "Now you can put on your hat, Cardinal." As a means of building up his physical strength and endurance and as a diversion, Philip learned the royal sport of hunting. As a youth he often hunted alone and killed wild boar with his sword. Though not tall or robust he was in good (although not excellent) health, and his natural hardiness, stemming from a strong will, suited him well for his princely duties. In him as in most princes was born constancy and a firmness of purpose. Because of his many virtues he was trusted implicitly. Fear neither disturbed nor disquieted him, and he could be trusted with both the conduct of war and the welfare of the state. He had a noble physiognomy, clear and well-formed with large bright-

blue eyes and had such a penetrating gaze that it commanded both reverence and respect. His handsome physical appearance, deserving of Empire, was augmented by his dignity, grace, and princely demeanor. Even when those who did not know him saw him in the woods, either alone or with others, they judged him worthy of respect and greeted him reverently. He had perfect eyesight and a keen ear for music, although he could not read music, nor did he know what kind of voice he had (for he never sang). He learned mathematics, understanding it even better than his engineers; he was ever aware of what was going on in his Empire, serving thus as a model for his successors and enabling him to rule his people more wisely. He demonstrated marvelous feats of memory, which was important because of the variety of tasks and the many ministers with whom he dealt. He increased his powers of memorization in order to keep his mind clear, and by putting details in their proper order and relationship, he could see more distinctly and clearly the principal lessons of history and morality. He underlined essential facts in his books, as can be seen in his library at San Lorenzo de Escorial. Careful to assimilate all that bore upon his office as king, he believed no precept too insignificant for him to learn, and like the Emperor Trajan, whom he studied, he was attentive to details. This practice aided him even more than divine inspiration in solving problems of war and peace and helped him lay down just laws for his subjects. His astute insights and Providence helped keep his subjects contented; his good judgment enabled him to balance the varying interests of his people and made him flexible in dealing with difficult foreign and domestic problems. He deployed military forces along his frontiers skillfully; he gave advice maturely; he acted firmly and was consistent in his deliberations; he maintained the military and waged war adeptly. He was strong in adversity, restrained in prosperity, and interpreted the work of the Divine in such a way as to keep his people from superstitious fear and licentiousness. He knew the inclinations of his vassals in advance, for their actions clearly revealed their intentions, thoughts, desires, and passions. He had special intuitive powers, the result of his training and upbringing, like special training given to animals that makes them different from those around them and changes their habits and disposition. Experience, the guide to understanding, ruled his will and made him the soul of prudence. Philip was completely in harmony with the institution of the monarchy and removed from the everyday affairs of the world and its vagaries. He knew it was dangerous to be inconsistent, to act by trial and error, and to make and unmake orders. He knew his provinces, cities, the countryside, its mountains and its rivers and much about military and civil government, finance, manufacturing, and taxes. Where he was unable to see things for himself, he used pictures and reports to attain an understanding of all his Empire, as Alexander the Great had wished to do. On May 1, 1539, just twenty days before his twelfth birthday, his mother, the deeply religious Portugese Empress, died; and in the absence of his father, Philip began to rule Spain with justice and divine zeal far superior to his years, proving that virtue is born in kings. He spoke solemnly, responded quickly and keenly; he perceived easily and observed closely. He was cautious in dealing with complex and difficult problems; wise and thorough in all his actions, he acted always as if his personal fortune were at stake. Surely the art of being king is the result of many influences on him who holds the office, but those who are trained from their youth in such activities are the best heirs to the throne. One day as the prince was leaving the palace, a woman came to him with tears in her eyes, requesting him to mitigate a death sentence imposed on her son for killing another man. Without moving from his horse, Philip inquired about the case from the presiding judge at the trial, who was in his party. Then said the king: "The sentence is a just one; however, in order that you benefit from having stopped to plead with me, I order the prisoner to be set free."

Philip II's Instructions to His Son, Philip III

PHILIP II, AS DICTATED TO HIS CONFESSOR, DIEGO DE YEPES

The following selection constitutes Philip's last words of advice to his son. Dictated shortly before the death of the king to his confessor, Diego de Yepes, these instructions indicate the deeply religious character of the Spanish monarch. They might also be interpreted as the credo by which Philip ruled or possibly as a list of mistakes he himself had made during his reign which he hoped his son would avoid. At the time he dictated these instructions, Philip was in great pain, suffering both from extreme rheumatism and boils which covered his entire body; undoubtedly he knew that he did not have long to live. This realization, the influence of his confessor, and the religious nature of Philip II all help to account for the somber, religious tone of the instructions.

STRIVE, my son, to love God with all your heart, for no one can be saved who does not love Him. Never commit mortal sin, rather suffer any kinds of torments than taint your soul with such a crime. Whenever you meet adversities, bear them in good spirit, and assume you deserve them. Whenever you enjoy good fortune, humbly give thanks to God; neither be proud when you ought to be humble, nor do evil when you ought to do good. Confess your sins often and seek out a wise confessor, who will instruct you in what course to avoid and what course to follow; and in your demeanor and attitude toward him, act in such a way that he will dare to admonish you and give you to understand the gravity of your sins. Hear Mass devoutly; do not listen there to fables or lies; neither be diverted in any way, but pray to God with mouth and heart, and do this particularly after the elevation of the Host.

Be of a pious, humane spirit toward the poor and afflicted, and favor them with everything that is within your power. If in your mind you contemplate doing something of importance, consult your confessor, or some wise man with high moral principles, in order to determine the most suitable course to follow. Let those who become your friends and confidants be good, virtuous, and respected men, whether they be laymen or clerics. Speak frankly with them. Always avoid vicious or slanderous conversation and discussion. Hear beneficial sermons by evangelical preachers, who condemn vice and are careful to honor and serve God. Take care also to earn forgiveness and indulgences. Cling to that which is good and abhor that which is evil. Wherever you may be, let no one in your presence dare to speak anything that may bring evil or harm to your fellowmen; neither should you, through gossip, blemish another's reputation, nor should you allow anyone in your presence to blaspheme or speak evil of God or His saints without punishing the culprit for his crime. Give thanks to God early for the ordinary blessings and graces of life that daily flow from His hand, so that you may thank Him also for His special blessings. In the administration of justice be fair and strict, adhering to what the law lays down without twisting it one way or the other. And never tire from hearing the complaints of the poor

From Luis Cabrera de Córdoba, *Felipe Segundo, Rey de España*, 4 vols. (Madrid, 1876), IV, pp. 390–392. [Editors' translation.]

but strive to learn the truth. If anyone has a complaint against you or feels himself abused by you, be more on his side than yours until the matter is determined, and thus the members of your council will be able to pronounce a more just sentence.

If you find that you possess something belonging to another, even though you received it from your forefathers as a legacy, return it without delay to its proper owner, if his ownership is unquestionable; and if it is questionable, let impartial judges clarify and determine the case without delay. You should take pride in according your subjects peace and justice; assure this particularly for priests and clergymen, that discord and injustice do not disturb them and their prayers to God for you and your kingdom; strive that they do not lack justice. You owe love, obedience, and reverence to your parents and elders. Ecclesiastical benefices should not be awarded except to the most worthy and to those who have none, and only upon the advice of wise counsellors. Do not wage war, especially against Christians, without great forethought and just cause; and if it is necessary to do so, let it be without harm to churches and innocent persons. If you are at war with another, whenever it is within your power, strive for peace; and if you are not directly involved, mediate between those at war in order that discord cease.

See to it that ministers of justice, councilmen, chief magistrates, and judges be virtuous and wise; and secretly inform yourself as to the administration of their offices. Always be obedient to the Roman Church and Supreme Pontiff, having him for your spiritual father. The expenses of your court should be moderate and conform to reason.

I admonish you my son, and solemnly charge you, if God should be pleased to take me from this life because of my infirmity, that throughout the kingdom, you hold Masses and offer up sacrifices for my soul. And finally, with all that a good and pious father can ask of and charge a good and pious son, this I entrust to you; and I pray God to keep you from all evil and to give you His grace always to do good, and to fulfill His wishes in all things, in a way that will be honorable for you, and that after this life, we all may see and contemplate and praise you in your goodness for all centuries. Amen.

THE DEVELOPMENT
OF THE BLACK LEGEND: THE ATTACKS
ON PHILIP II's CHARACTER

The Apologia of 1580 of William of Orange

PRINCE OF THE HOUSE OF ORANGE-NASSAU

At the age of thirty-four, William of Nassau, Prince of Orange (1533–1584), better known to history as William the Silent, became the leader of the people of the Dutch Netherlands in their revolt against Philip II. William has been called by some "the wisest, gentlest, and bravest man who ever led a nation," and by others a "deceitful, self-seeking politician, and traitor." The Dutch referred to him as "the Father of his People," but to the Spanish he incarnated the evils of the Reformation, the cunning of the Flemings, and the ingratitude of an upstart. William's character represents a blending of both virtues and vices, making him, like Philip II, the subject of heated discussion to this day. The selection from his *Apology* of 1580, reprinted below, displays the worst aspects of William's personality: his vindictiveness, vanity, and lack of candor. But it must be remembered that he was fighting, not only for his political future, but for his very life and in doing so obviously exaggerated and often deliberately misread historical facts. As a result, William's *Apology* has served historians hostile to Philip as an ever-fresh source of the Black Legend.

BUT my accuser [Philip II] will not find it so easy to vindicate his own conduct from . . . odious imputation. Read my defence which I published some years ago; and you will perceive to which of us belongs the appellation of hypocrite and deceiver. In that defence, there are copies of letters which I received from him, filled with professions of friendship and regard, at the very time when, as appears from the sequel, he had doomed me to destruction. . . . He seems not to have remembered the common maxim, that whoever ventures to accuse another, ought to be well assured that he himself is innocent. And yet is not this King, who has endeavoured to stigma-tise my lawful marriage with infamy, the husband of his own niece? It will be said by his partisans, that he previously obtained a dispensation from the pope. But does not the voice of nature cry aloud against such an incestuous conjunction? And in order to make room for this marriage, is it not true, that he put to death his former wife, the mother of his children, the daughter and sister of the kings of France? I say not this, prompted by my resentment, rashly and at random. I assert, that in France there is evidence of the horrid deed of which I now accuse him.

It was not a single murder that was perpetrated for the sake of this extraordinary

From: "An Abstract of the Apology or Vindication of the Prince of Orange against Philip's Proscription," in Robert Watson, *The History of the Reign of Philip the Second, King of Spain* (London, 1794), III, pp. 357–360, 364–365, and 366–372.

marriage. His son too, his only son, was sacrificed, in order to furnish the pope with a pretext for so unusual a dispensation; which was granted, in order to prevent the Spanish monarchy from being left without a male heir. This was the true cause of the death of Don Carlos, against whom some misdemeanours were alleged; but not a single crime sufficient to justify his condemnation, much less to vindicate a father for imbruing his hands in the blood of his son. And if Don Carlos was in reality guilty of crimes deserving death, ought not an appeal to have been made to us, his future subjects? Did the right of judging, and pronouncing sentence of death against the heir of such extensive dominions, belong to Spanish friars and inquisitors, the obsequious slaves of the father's tyranny?

But I shall hasten to conclude this Apology, after offering some remarks concerning the nature of the sentence that has been pronounced against me. It is in this part of the edict of proscription, that the compiler, whether the King himself, or some ignoble instrument of his tyranny, has employed all the thunder and lightning of his eloquence. But I thank God, it intimidates me no more than the anathemas of Clement VII intimidated my kinsman prince Philibert, when he besieged and took the pontiff prisoner in his castle of St. Angelo, after the proofs which I have given, that I fear not all the power which my adversary is possessed of; and after contending for so many years against his best generals, with numerous armies under their command, it was weak in him to expect to frighten me with the high-sounding terms of this proscription. I have less reason now, than formerly, to dread the attempts of those abandoned wretches, whom he has endeavoured to instigate against me. For I am not ignorant, that before this time he has bargained with poisoners, and other murderers, to deprive me of my life. He has now given me a public warning of his bloody design. And with the divine assistance, and the vigilance of my friends, I trust, that notwithstanding his diabolical

machinations, my life shall be preserved so long as the prosperity and interest of this people, to whose service I have devoted it, shall require.

My confidence on this head is greatly augmented by reflecting upon the indignation, which I cannot doubt will be generally excited by that extraordinary method of proceeding against me, which my adversary has adopted. For there is not, I am persuaded, a nation or prince in Europe, by whom it will not be thought dishonourable and barbarous, thus publicly to authorise and encourage murder; except the Spaniards, and their King, who have been long estranged from every sentiment of honour and humanity. In having recourse to private assassinations against a declared and open enemy, does not this mighty monarch confess his despair of being able to subdue me by force of arms? Does he not give a testimony in my behalf, and discover that he dreads the efforts which I may make against him? Is it not weak and mean, to make publicly so pusillanimous an acknowledgment? But the weakness and meanness of his conduct is not greater than the absurdity of his choice of the rewards, which he holds forth to those who shall execute his bloody purpose. For it is not money only that he offers them, but nobility and honour; as if a regard to honour could influence a man capable of perpetrating a deed held in universal detestation. And if any person already possessed of nobility were to pollute himself by so foul an action, would not his nobility from that moment be annihilated? Would not all society and connection with him be held dishonourable?

Even my adversary himself seems to have been in some measure sensible of the truth of this, and therefore he addresses himself more particularly to criminals and malefactors, as those who are most likely to comply with his request. "And in order," says he, "that his destruction may be the more effectually and speedily accomplished, we, desirous of punishing vice, and rewarding virtue, promise on the word of a king, and as the minister of God, that if any person shall be found possessed of courage and public spirit sufficient to animate him to the execution of this decree, and to free us from the aforesaid pest of society, we shall order to be delivered to him, either in land or money as he shall incline, the sum of twenty-five thousand crowns; and if he shall have committed any crime, however enormous, we promise to grant him our royal pardon; and if he be not already noble, we hereby confer nobility upon him, and likewise on all those who shall aid and assist him." Is not this, in plain terms, calling on every desperate wretch, every outcast from society, to assist him in the execution of his design? No crime, however enormous, but shall be pardoned; no criminal, however detestable, but shall be crowned with honour. Does this king deserve the title which he assumes, a minister of God, who thus confounds the distinction between vice and virtue; and thus publicly avows his willingness to bestow the highest rewards and honours upon men defiled with the most abominable crimes? Have I not ground to rejoice in being persecuted by one whose conscience allows him to have recourse to such unhallowed means? And is not such depravity of sentiment in my accuser, a testimony in behalf of my integrity?

I have now said all that seems necessary to vindicate my character from those false aspersions which are thrown upon it in this proscription. Many things which I might have said, I have purposely omitted. Had I descended to a particular account of the cruelty, accompanied with a contempt of the most sacred obligations, which has been exercised by my accuser over this unhappy people, I should never have come to a conclusion. But with you there can be occasion for giving a more particular detail. You have been spectators of the horrid scene, and have borne your share of those oppressions, which would fail to be described.

But before I conclude, I must entreat you to reflect seriously upon the means to which our enemy finds it necessary to have recourse, in order to accomplish his designs. This infamous proscription, joined to the pains which he and his ministers continually employ to create divisions among the provinces, shows clearly that he now despairs of enslaving us by force of arms, while we remain united.

It is indeed against me chiefly, at this time, that his designs are directed. "Were I removed," he says, "either by death or banishment, tranquillity would be restored." You will easily conceive what tranquillity he means, if you call to mind your condition, before I returned into the Netherlands, when you groaned under the tyranny of the Duke of Alva. Would to heaven that by my banishment or death you could be delivered from your calamities! My enemy should not, in that case, find it necessary to employ poisoners and assassins to destroy me. You all know how often I have exposed myself to danger in your defence. I leave it to you, to whom alone it belongs, to determine, whether my life and presence be repugnant or conducive to the interest of the provinces. To you only, and not to the King of Spain, I am accountable for my conduct. You have full authority (and I pledge myself to submit to it) to dispose, as you shall incline, either of my person, or of my life. Interpose that authority with which I acknowledge you to be invested, and give orders either for my departure from among you, or for my death; if you judge either the one or the other for the general good. But if, on the contrary, my past conduct has convinced you, as I trust it has, of the sincerity of my zeal and attachment; or if my long experience gives you confidence in my ability for conducting your affairs, I shall still continue to employ in your service, the talents which I possess, hoping that you will listen to the earnest exhortations which I have given you, to maintain harmony and concord in the state; and exert yourselves strenuously for the defence of this people, whom you have undertaken to protect; depending on the favour of the Almighty, that your endeavours for this end shall be attended with success.

An Eighteenth-Century View of
Philip II's Character

ROBERT WATSON

Robert Watson (1730?–1781), a Scottish divine and professor, was educated at St. Andrews, Glasgow, and Edinburgh Universities. In 1777 he published his two-volume *History of Philip II of Spain,* which received wide critical acclaim and achieved eminence in late eighteenth-century literary circles. So great was the demand for this history, that it reached its seventh edition by 1812 and was translated into French, German, and Dutch. The selection reprinted below betrays the strong anti-clerical bias typical of the eighteenth century.

No character was ever drawn by different historians in more opposite colours than that of Philip; and yet considering the length and activity of his reign, there is none which it should seem would be more easy to ascertain. From the facts recorded in the preceding history, we cannot doubt that he possessed, in an eminent degree, penetration, vigilance, and a capacity for government. His eyes were continually open upon every part of his extensive dominions. He entered into every branch of administration; watched over the conduct of his ministers with unwearied attention; and in his choice both of them and of his generals, discovered a considerable share of sagacity. He had at all times a composed and settled countenance, and never appeared to be either elated or depressed. His temper was the most imperious, and his looks and demeanour were haughty and severe; yet among his Spanish subjects, he was of easy access; listened patiently to their representations and complaints; and where his ambition and bigotry did not interfere, was generally willing to redress their grievances. When we have said this much in his praise, we have said all that justice requires, or truth permits. It is indeed impossible to suppose that he was insincere in his zeal for religion. But as his religion was of the most corrupt kind, it served to increase the natural depravity of his disposition; and not only allowed, but even prompted him to commit the most odious and shocking crimes. Although a prince in the bigoted age of Philip might be persuaded that the interest of religion would be advanced by falsehood and persecution; yet it might be expected, that, in a virtuous prince, the sentiments of honour and humanity would, on some occasions, triumph over the dictates of superstition: but of this triumph, there occurs not a single instance in the reign of Philip; who, without hesitation, violated his most sacred obligations as often as religion afforded him a pretense; and under that pretense exercised for many years the most unrelenting cruelty, without reluctance or remorse. His ambition, which was exorbitant; his resentment, which was implacable; his arbitrary temper, which would submit to no control; concurred with his bigoted zeal for the Catholic religion, and carried the sanguinary spirit, which that religion was calculated to inspire, to a greater height in Philip, than it ever attained in any other prince of that, or of any former or succeeding age.

From Robert Watson, *The History of the Reign of Philip the Second, King of Spain,* 3 vols. (London, 1794), III, pp. 334–338.

Some historians have distinguished this prince by the title of Philip the Prudent, and have represented him as the wisest, as well as the most religious prince, that ever filled the Spanish throne. But it is questionable, whether he be entitled to praise on account of his prudence, any more than on account of his religion. In the beginning of his reign, he discovered great caution in his military enterprise; and, on some occasions, made even greater preparations than were necessary to insure success. But his ambition, his resentment, and his abhorrence of the Protestants were too violent to suffer him to act conformably to the dictates of sound policy and prudence. He might have prevented the revolt of his Dutch and Flemish subjects, if, after the reformation in the Netherlands was suppressed by the Dutchess of Parma, he had left the reins of government in the hands of that wise princess, and had not sent so odious a tyrant as the Duke of Alva to enslave them. He might, after the defeat of the Prince of Orange, have rivetted the chains of slavery about their necks, and gradually accustomed them to the yoke; if, by engaging in too many expensive enterprises, he had not exhausted his exchequer, and made it in some measure necessary for Alva to impose the taxes of the tenth and twentieth pennies, for the maintenance of his troops. He might, through the great abilities of the Duke of Parma, have again reduced the revolted provinces to obedience, if he had not conceived the wild ambition of subduing England and acquiring the sovereignty of France. His armies, in the latter part of his reign, were never sufficiently numerous to execute the various enterprises which he undertook; yet they were much more numerous than he was able to support. Few years past in which they did not mutiny for want of pay. And Philip suffered greater prejudice from the disorders and devastation which his own troops committed, than he received from the arms of his enemies. Against his attempts on England and France, his wisest counsellors remonstrated in the strongest terms. And prudence certainly required that, previously to any attack upon the dominions of others, he should have secured possession of his own. Yet so great was his illusion, that rather than delay the execution of those schemes which his resentment and ambition had suggested, he chose to run the risk of losing the fruits of all the victories which the Duke of Parma had obtained; and having left defenseless the provinces which had submitted to his authority, he thereby afforded an opportunity to the revolted provinces, of establishing their power, on so firm a foundation, as could not be shaken by the whole strength of the Spanish monarchy, exerted against it for more than fifty years.

The Incarnation of Evil

JOHN LOTHROP MOTLEY

John Lothrop Motley (1814–1877) was a New Englander of vast learning and unusual abilities. Graduated from Harvard University at the age of seventeen, Motley studied both law and literature in Germany at the University of Göttingen and the University of Berlin. After a period of travel he settled down to practice law in Boston, but this occupation was only a mask for his literary efforts. Two novels written in the 1830's proved undistinguished, but in the next decade when he turned his attention to history, Motley was more successful. Motley's focus was Dutch history. Attracted by the similarity between the development of the United Provinces of the Netherlands and that of the United States, he saw both nations as having achieved independence and freedom against the forces of despotism and oppression. His first work, *The Rise of the Dutch Republic*, was published in 1856 and received wide popular acclaim. More volumes followed, including the *History of the United Netherlands*, from which this selection has been taken. Despite his sojourn in Germany, Motley was not influenced by the new Rankean school of historical investigation. He wrote didactic history with strong personal prejudices. One observer has stated that his work showed "more learning than insight" and "more enthusiasm than sobriety."

THESE volumes will have been written in vain if it be now necessary to recall to my readers the leading events in the history of the man who had thus left the world where, almost invisible himself, he had so long played a leading part. It may not be entirely useless, however, to throw a parting glance at a character which it has been one of the main objects of this work, throughout its whole course, to portray. My theme has been the reign of Philip II because, as the less is included in the greater, the whole of that reign, with the exception of a few episodes, is included in the vast movement out of which the Republic of the United Netherlands was born and the assailed independence of France and England consolidated. The result of Philip's efforts to establish a universal monarchy was to hasten the decline of the empire which he had inherited, by aggravating the evils which had long made that downfall inevitable.

It is from no abstract hatred to monarchy that I have dwelt with emphasis upon the crimes of this king, and upon the vices of the despotic system, as illustrated during his lifetime. It is not probable that the military, monarchical system — founded upon conquests achieved by barbarians and pirates of a distant epoch over an effete civilization and over antique institutions of intolerable profligacy — will soon come to an end in the older world. And it is the business of Europeans so to deal with the institutions of their inheritance or their choice as to ensure their steady melioration and to provide for the highest interests of the people. It matters comparatively little by what name a government is called, so long as the intellectual and moral development of mankind, and the maintenance of justice among individuals, are its leading principles. A government, like an individual, may remain far below its ideal; but, without an ideal, governments and individ-

From John Lothrop Motley, *History of the United Netherlands*, 4 vols. (New York, 1867), III, pp. 512–517 and 532–543.

13

uals are alike contemptible. It is tyranny only — whether individual or popular — that utters its feeble sneers at the ideologists, as if mankind were brutes to whom instincts were all in all and ideas nothing. Where intellect and justice are enslaved by that unholy trinity — Force, Dogma, and Ignorance — the tendency of governments, and of those subjected to them, must of necessity be retrograde and downward.

There can be little doubt to those who observe the movements of mankind during the course of the fourteen centuries since the fall of the Roman Empire — a mere fragment of human history — that its progress, however concealed or impeded, and whether for weal or woe, is towards democracy; for it is the tendency of science to liberate and to equalize the physical and even the intellectual forces of humanity. A horse and a suit of armour would now hardly enable the fortunate possessor of such advantages to conquer a kingdom, nor can wealth and learning be monopolised in these latter days by a favoured few. Yet veneration for a crown and a privileged church — as if without them and without their close connection with each other law and religion were impossible — makes hereditary authority sacred to great masses of mankind in the old world. The obligation is the more stringent, therefore, on men thus set apart as it were by primordial selection for ruling and instructing their fellow-creatures, to keep their edicts and their practice in harmony with divine justice. For these rules cannot be violated with impunity during a long succession of years, and it is usually left for a comparatively innocent generation to atone for the sins of their forefathers. If history does not teach this it teaches nothing, and as the rules of morality, whether for individuals or for nations, are simple and devoid of mystery, there is the less excuse for governments which habitually and cynically violate the eternal law.

Among self-evident truths not one is more indisputable than that which, in the immortal words of our Declaration of Independence, asserts the right of every human being to life, liberty, and the pursuit of happiness; but the only happiness that can be recognized by a true statesman as the birthright of mankind is that which comes from intellectual and moral development, and from the subjugation of the brutal instincts.

A system according to which clowns remain clowns through all the ages, unless when extraordinary genius or fortunate accident enables an exceptional individual to overleap the barrier of caste, necessarily retards the result to which the philosopher looks forward with perfect faith.

For us, whose business it is to deal with, and, so far as human fallibility will permit, to improve our inevitable form of government — which may degenerate into the most intolerable of polities unless we are ever mindful that it is yet in its rudimental condition; that, although an immense step had been taken in the right direction by the abolition of caste, the divorce of Church and State, and the limitation of intrusion by either on the domain of the individual, it is yet only a step from which, without eternal vigilance, a falling back is very easy; and that here, more than in other lands, ignorance of the scientific and moral truths on which national happiness and prosperity depend, deserves bitter denunciation — for us it is wholesome to confirm our faith in democracy, and to justify our hope that the People will prove itself equal to the awful responsibility of self-government by an occasional study of the miseries which the opposite system is capable of producing. It is for this reason that the reign of the sovereign whose closing moments have just been recorded is especially worthy of a minute examination, and I still invite a parting glance at the spectacle thus presented, before the curtain falls.

The Spanish monarchy in the reign of Philip II was not only the most considerable empire then existing, but probably the most powerful and extensive empire that had ever been known. Certainly never before had so great an agglomeration of distinct and separate sovereignties been the result of accident. For it was owing to a series of accidents — in the common acceptation of that term — that Philip governed so mighty a realm. According to the principle that vast tracts of the earth's surface, with the human beings feeding upon them, were transferable in fee-simple from one man or woman to another by marriage, inheritance, or gift, a heterogeneous collection of kingdoms, principalities, provinces, and wildernesses had been consolidated, without geographical continuity, into an artificial union — the populations differing from each other as much as human beings can differ, in race, language, institutions, and historical traditions, and resembling each other in little, save in being the property alike of the same fortunate individual.

Thus the dozen kingdoms of Spain, the seventeen provinces of the Netherlands, the kingdoms of the Two Sicilies, the duchy of Milan, and certain fortresses and districts of Tuscany, in Europe; the kingdom of Barbary, the coast of Guinea, and an indefinite and unmeasured expanse of other territory, in Africa; the controlling outposts and cities all along the coast of the two Indian peninsulas, with as much of the country as it seemed good to occupy, the straits and the great archipelagoes, so far as they had been visited by Europeans, in Asia; Peru, Brazil, Mexico, the Antilles — the whole recently discovered fourth quarter of the world in short, from the "Land of Fire" in the South to the frozen regions of the North — as much territory as the Spanish and Portuguese sea-captains could circumnavigate and the pope in the plentitude of his power and his generosity could bestow on his fortunate son, in America; all this enormous proportion of the habitable globe was the private property of Philip, who was the son of Charles, who was the son of Joanna, who was the daughter of Isabella, whose husband was Ferdinand. By what seems to us the most whimsical of political arrangements, the Papuan islander, the Calabrian peasant, the Amsterdam merchant, the semi-civilized Aztec, the Moor of Barbary, the Castilian grandee, the roving Comanche, the Guinea negro, the Indian Brahmin, found themselves — could they but have known it — fellow-citizens of one commonwealth. Statutes of family descent, aided by fraud, force, and chicane, had annexed the various European sovereignties to the crown of Spain; the genius of a Genoese sailor had given to it the New World, and more recently the conquest of Portugal, torn from hands not strong enough to defend the national independence, had vested in the same sovereignty those Oriental possessions which were due to the enterprise of Vasco de Gama, his comrades and successors. The voyager, setting forth from the straits of Gibraltar, circumnavigating the African headlands and Cape Comorin, and sailing through the Molucca channel and past the isles which bore the name of Philip in the Eastern sea, gave the hand at last to his adventurous comrade, who, starting from the same point, and following westward in the track of Magellaens and under the Southern Cross, coasted the shore of Patagonia, and threaded his path through unmapped and unnumbered clusters of islands in the Western Pacific; and during this spanning of the earth's whole circumference not an inch of land or water was traversed that was not the domain of Philip.

For the sea, too, was his as well as the dry land.

From Borneo to California the great ocean was but a Spanish lake, as much the king's private property as his fish-ponds at the Escorial with their carp and perch. No subjects but his dared to navigate those sacred waters. Not a common highway of the world's commerce, but a private path for the gratification of one human being's vanity, had thus been laid out by the bold navigators of the sixteenth century.

It was for the Dutch rebels to try conclusions upon this point, as they had done upon so many others, with the master of the land and sea. The opening scenes, therefore, in the great career of maritime adventure and discovery by which these republicans were to make themselves famous will soon engage the reader's attention.

Thus the causes of what is called the greatness of Spain are not far to seek. Spain was not a nation, but a temporary and factitious conjunction of several nations, which it was impossible to fuse into a permanent whole, but over whose united resources a single monarch for a time disposed. And the very concentration of these vast and unlimited powers, fortuitous as it was, in this single hand, inspiring the individual, not unnaturally, with a consciousness of superhuman grandeur, impelled him to those frantic and puerile efforts to achieve the impossible which resulted in the downfall of Spain. The man who inherited so much material greatness believed himself capable of destroying the invisible but omnipotent spirit of religious and political liberty in the Netherlands, of trampling out the national existence of France and of England, and of annexing those realms to his empire. It has been my task to relate, with much minuteness, how miserably his efforts failed.

His power was absolute. With this single phrase one might as well dismiss any attempt at specification. He made war or peace at will with foreign nations. He had power of life and death over all his subjects. He had unlimited control of their worldly goods. And he claimed supreme jurisdiction over their religious opinions also, he was master of their minds, bodies, and estates. As a matter of course, he nominated and removed at will every executive functionary, every judge, every magistrate, every military or civil officer; and moreover, he not only selected, according to the license tacitly conceded to him by the pontiff, every archbishop, bishop, and other Church dignitary, but, through his great influence at Rome, he named most of the cardinals, and thus controlled the election of the popes. The whole machinery of society, political, ecclesiastical, military, was in his single hand. There was a show

of provincial privilege here and there in different parts of Spain, but it was but the phantom of that ancient municipal liberty which it had been the especial care of his father and his great-grandfather to destroy. Most patiently did Philip, by his steady inactivity, bring about the decay of the last ruins of free institutions in the peninsula. The councils and legislative assemblies were convoked and then wearied out in waiting for that royal assent to their propositions and transactions, which was deferred intentionally, year after year, and never given. Thus the time of the deputies was consumed in accomplishing infinite nothing, until the moment arrived when the monarch, without any violent stroke of state, could feel safe in issuing decrees and pragmatic edicts; thus reducing the ancient legislative and consultative bodies to nullity, and substituting the will of an individual for a constitutional fabric. To criticise the expenses of government or to attempt interference with the increase of taxation became a sorry farce. The forms remained in certain provinces after the life had long since fled. Only in Aragon had the ancient privileges seemed to defy the absolute authority of the monarch; and it was reserved for Antonio Perez to be the cause of their final extirpation. The grinning skulls of the Chief Justice of that kingdom and of the boldest and noblest advocates and defenders of the national liberties, exposed for years in the marketplace, with the record of their death-sentence attached, informed the Spaniards, in language which the most ignorant could read, that the crime of defending a remnant of human freedom and constitutional law was sure to draw down condign punishment. It was the last time in that age that even the ghost of extinct liberty was destined to revisit the soil of Spain. It mattered not that the immediate cause for pursuing Perez was his successful amour with the king's mistress, nor that the crime of which he was formally accused was the deadly offence of Calvinism, rather than his intrigue with the Eboli and his assassination of Escovedo; for it was in the natural and simple sequence of events that the last vestige of law or freedom should be obliterated wherever Philip could vindicate his sway. It must be admitted, too, that the king seized this occasion to strike a decisive blow with a promptness very different from his usual artistic sluggishness. Rarely has a more terrible epigram been spoken by man than the royal words which constituted the whole trial and sentence of the Chief Justice of Aragon, for the crime of defending the law of his country: "You will take John of Lanuza, and you will have his head cut off." This was the end of the magistrate and of the constitution which he had defended.

His power was unlimited. A man endowed with genius and virtue, and possessing the advantages of a consummate education, could have perhaps done little more than attempt to mitigate the general misery, and to remove some of its causes. For it is one of the most pernicious dogmas of the despotic system, and the one which the candid student of history soonest discovers to be false, that the masses of mankind are to look to any individual, however exalted by birth or intellect, for their redemption. Woe to the world if the nations are never to learn that their fate is and ought to be in their own hands; that their institutions, whether liberal or despotic, are the result of the national biography and of the national character, not the work of a few individuals whose names have been preserved by capricious Accident as heroes and legislators. Yet there is no doubt that, while comparatively powerless for good, the individual despot is capable of almost infinite mischief. There have been few men known to history who have been able to accomplish by their own exertions so vast an amount of evil as the king who had just died. If Philip possessed a single virtue, it has eluded the conscientious research of the writer of these pages. If there are vices — as possibly there are — from which he was exempt, it is because it is not permitted to human nature to attain perfection even

in evil. The only plausible explanation — for palliation there is none — of his infamous career is that the man really believed himself, not a king, but a god. He was placed so high above his fellow-creatures as, in good faith perhaps, to believe himself incapable of doing wrong; so that, whether indulging his passions or enforcing throughout the world his religious and political dogmas, he was ever conscious of embodying divine inspirations and elemental laws. When providing for the assassination of a monarch, or commanding the massacre of a townful of Protestants; when trampling on every oath by which a human being can bind himself; when laying desolate with fire and sword, during more than a generation, the provinces which he had inherited as his private property, or in carefully maintaining the flames of civil war in foreign kingdoms which he hoped to acquire; while maintaining over all Christendom a gigantic system of bribery, corruption, and espionage, keeping the noblest names of England and Scotland on his pension-lists of traitors, and impoverishing his exchequer with the wages of iniquity paid in France to men of all degrees, from princes of blood like Guise and Mayenne down to the obscurest of country squires, he ever felt that these base or bloody deeds were not crimes, but the simple will of the godhead of which he was a portion. He never doubted that the extraordinary theological system which he spent his life in enforcing with fire and sword was right, for it was a part of himself. The Holy Inquisition, thoroughly established as it was in his ancestral Spain, was a portion of the regular working machinery by which his absolute kingship and his superhuman will expressed themselves. A tribunal which performed its functions with a celerity, certainty, and invisibility resembling the attributes of Omnipotence; which, like the pestilence, entered palace or hovel at will, and which smote the wretch guilty or suspected of heresy with a precision against which no human ingenuity or sympathy could guard — such an institution could not but be dear to his heart. It was inevitable that the extension and perpetuation of what he deemed its blessings throughout his dominions should be his settled purpose. Spain was governed by an established terrorism. It is a mistake to suppose that Philip was essentially beloved in his native land, or that his religious and political system was heartily accepted because consonant to the national character. On the contrary, as has been shown, a very large proportion of the inhabitants were either secretly false to the Catholic faith, or descended at least from those who had expiated their hostility to it with their lives. But the Grand Inquisitor was almost as awful a personage as the king or the pope. His familiars were in every village and at every fireside, and from their fangs there was no escape. Millions of Spaniards would have rebelled against the crown or accepted the reformed religion, had they not been perfectly certain of being burned or hanged at the slightest movement in such a direction. The popular force in the course of the political combinations of centuries seemed at last to have been eliminated. The nobles, exempt from taxation, which crushed the people to the earth, were the enemies rather than the chieftains and champions of the lower classes in any possible struggle with a crown to which they were united by ties of interest as well as of affection, while the great churchmen, too, were the immediate dependants and of course the firm supporters of the king. Thus the people, without natural leaders, without organisation, and themselves divided into two mutually hostile sections, were opposed by every force in the State. Crown, nobility, and clergy; all the wealth and all that there was of learning, were banded together to suppress the democratic principle. But even this would hardly have sufficed to extinguish every spark of liberty, had it not been for the potent machinery of the Inquisition; nor could that perfection of terrorism have become an established institution but for the extraordinary mixture of pride and superstition of which the

national character had been, in the course of the national history, compounded. The Spanish portion of the people hated the nobles, whose petty exactions and oppressions were always visible; but they had a reverential fear of the unseen monarch, as the representative both of the great unsullied Christian nation to which the meanest individual was proud to belong, and of the God of wrath who had decreed the extermination of all unbelievers. The "accursed" portion of the people were sufficiently disloyal at heart, but were too much crushed by oppression and contempt to imagine themselves men. As to the Netherlanders, they did not fight originally for independence. It was not until after a quarter of a century of fighting that they ever thought of renouncing their allegiance to Philip. They fought to protect themselves against being taxed by the king without the consent of those constitutional assemblies which he had sworn to maintain, and to save themselves and their children from being burned alive if they dared to read the Bible. Independence followed after nearly a half-century of fighting, but it would never have been obtained, or perhaps demanded, had those grievances of the people been redressed.

Of this perfect despotism Philip was thus the sole administrator. Certainly he looked upon his mission with seriousness, and was industrious in performing his royal functions. But this earnestness and seriousness were, in truth, his darkest vices; for the most frivolous voluptuary that ever wore a crown would never have compassed a thousandth part of the evil which was Philip's life-work. It was because he was a believer in himself, and in what he called his religion, that he was enabled to perpetrate such a long catalogue of crimes. When an humble malefactor is brought before an ordinary court of justice, it is not often, in any age or country, that he escapes the pillory or the gallows because, from his own point of view, his actions, instead of being criminal, have been commendable, and because the multitude and continuity of his offences prove him to have been sincere. And because anointed monarchs are amendable to no human tribunal, save to that terrible assize which the People, bursting its chain from time to time in the course of the ages, sets up for the trial of its oppressors, and which is called Revolution, it is the more important for the great interests of humanity that before the judgment-seat of History a crown should be no protection to its wearer. There is no plea to the jurisdiction of history, if history be true to itself.

As for the royal criminal called Philip II, his life is his arraignment, and these volumes will have been written in vain if a specification is now required.

Homicide such as was hardly ever compassed before by one human being was committed by Philip when in the famous edict of 1568 he sentenced every man, woman, and child in the Netherlands to death. That the whole of this population, three millions or more, were not positively destroyed was because no human energy could suffice to execute the diabolical decree. But Alva, toiling hard, accomplished much of this murderous work. By the aid of the "Council of Blood," and of the sheriffs and executioners of the Holy Inquisition, he was able sometimes to put eight hundred human beings to death in a single week for the crimes of Protestantism or of opulence, and at the end of half a dozen years he could boast of having strangled, drowned, burned, or beheaded somewhat more than eighteen thousand of his fellow-creatures. These were some of the non-combatant victims; for of the tens of thousands who perished during his administration alone, in siege and battle, no statistical record has been preserved.

In face of such wholesale crimes, of these forty years of bloodshed, it is superfluous to refer to such isolated misdeeds as his repeated attempts to procure the assassination of the Prince of Orange, crowned at last by the success of Balthazar Gerard, nor to his persistent efforts to poison the Queen of England; for the enunciation of all these murders or attempts at murder would require a repetition of the story which it has been one of the main purposes of these volumes to recite.

For indeed it seems like mere railing to specify his crimes. Their very magnitude and unbroken continuity, together with their impunity, give them almost the appearance of inevitable phenomena. The horrible monotony of his career stupefies the mind until it is ready to accept the principle of evil as the fundamental law of the world.

His robberies, like his murders, were colossal. The vast system of confiscation set up in the Netherlands was sufficient to reduce unnumbered innocent families to beggary, although powerless to break the spirit of civil and religious liberty or to pay the expenses of subjugating a people. Not often in the world's history have so many thousand individuals been plundered by a foreign tyrant for no crime, save that they were rich enough to be worth robbing. For it can never be too often repeated that those confiscations and extortions were perpetrated upon Catholics as well as Protestants, monarchists as well as rebels; the possession of property making proof of orthodoxy or of loyalty well-nigh impossible.

Falsehood was the great basis of the king's character, which perhaps derives its chief importance, as a political and psychological study, from this very fact. It has been shown throughout the whole course of this history, by the evidence of his most secret correspondence, that he was false, most of all, to those to whom he gave what he called his heart. Granvelle, Alva, Don John, Alexander Farnese, all those, in short, who were deepest in his confidence experienced in succession his entire perfidy, while each in turn was sacrificed to his master's sleepless suspicion. The pope himself was often as much the dupe of the Catholic monarch's faithlessness as the vilest heretic had ever been. Could the great schoolmaster of iniquity for the sovereigns and politicians of the south have lived to witness the practice of the monarch who had most laid to heart the precepts of the "Prince," he would have felt that he had not written in vain, and that his great paragon of successful falsehood, Ferdinand of Aragon, had been surpassed by the great grandson. For the ideal perfection of perfidy, foreshadowed by the philosopher who died in the year of Philip's birth, was thoroughly embodied at last by this potentate. Certainly Nicholas Machiavelli could have hoped for no more docile pupil. That all men are vile, that they are liars, scoundrels, poltroons, and idiots alike — ever ready to deceive and yet easily to be duped, and that he only is fit to be king who excels his kind in the arts of deception; by this great maxim of the Florentine, Philip was ever guided. And those well-known texts of hypocrisy, strewn by the same hand, had surely not fallen on stony ground when received into Philip's royal soul.

Often it is necessary, in order to maintain power, to act contrary to faith, contrary to charity, contrary to humanity, contrary to religion. . . . A prince ought therefore to have great care that from his mouth nothing should ever come that is not filled with those five qualities, and that to see and hear him he should appear all piety, all faith, all integrity, all humanity, all religion. And nothing is more necessary than to seem to have this last-mentioned quality. . . . Everyone sees what you seem, few perceive what you are.

Surely this handbook of cant had been Philip's *vade mecum* through his life's pilgrimage.

It is at least a consolation to reflect that a career controlled by such principles came to an ignominious close. Had the mental capacity of this sovereign been equal to his criminal intent, even greater woe might have befallen the world. But his intellect was less than mediocre. His passion for the bureau, his slavery to routine, his puerile ambition personally to superintend details which could have been a thousand times better administered by

subordinates, proclaimed every day the narrowness of his mind. His diligence in reading, writing, and commenting upon despatches may excite admiration only when there has been no opportunity of judging of his labours by personal inspection. Those familiar with the dreary displays of his penmanship must admit that such work could have been at least as well done by a copying clerk of average capacity. His ministers were men of respectable ability, but he imagined himself, as he advanced in life, far superior to any counsellor that he could possibly select, and was accustomed to consider himself the first statesman in the world.

His reign was a thorough and disgraceful failure. Its opening scene was the treaty of Cateau Cambresis, by which a triumph over France had been achieved for him by the able generals and statesmen of his father, so humiliating and complete as to make every French soldier or politician gnash his teeth. Its conclusion was the treaty of Vervins with the same power, by which the tables were completely turned, and which was as utterly disgraceful to Spain as that of Cateau Cambresis had been to France. He had spent his life in fighting with the spirit of the age — that invincible power of which he had not the faintest conception — while the utter want of adaptation of his means to his ends often bordered, not on the ludicrous, but the insane.

He attempted to reduce the free Netherlands to slavery and to papacy. Before his death they had expanded into an independent republic, with a policy founded upon religious toleration and the rights of man. He had endeavoured all his life to exclude the Bearnese from his heritage and to place himself or his daughter on the vacant throne; before his death Henry IV was the most powerful and popular sovereign that had ever reigned in France. He had sought to invade and to conquer England, and to dethrone and assassinate its queen. But the queen outwitted, outgeneraled, and out-lived him; English soldiers and sailors, assisted by their Dutch comrades in arms, accomplished on the shores of Spain what the Invincible Armada had in vain essayed against England and Holland; while England, following thenceforth the opposite system to that of absolutism and the Inquisition, became, after centuries of struggles towards the right, the most powerful, prosperous, and enlightened kingdom in the world.

His exchequer, so full when he ascended the throne as to excite the awe of contemporary financiers, was reduced before his death to a net income of some four millions of dollars. His armies, which had been the wonder of the age in the earlier period of his reign for discipline, courage, and every quality on which military efficiency depends, were in his later years a horde of starving, rebellious brigands, more formidable to their commanders than to the foe. Mutiny was the only organised military institution that was left in his dominions, while the Spanish Inquisition, which it was the fell purpose of his life from youth upwards to establish over the world, became a loathsome and impossible nuisance everywhere but in its natal soil.

If there be such a thing as historical evidence, then is Philip II convicted before the tribunal of impartial posterity of every crime charged in his indictment. He lived seventy-one years and three months, he reigned forty-three years. He endured the martyrdom of his last illness with the heroism of a saint, and died in the certainty of immortal bliss as the reward of his life of evil.

THE RETREAT FROM MORALISM:
REAPPRAISALS OF PHILIP II

The Dilatory Hermit of the Escorial

LEOPOLD VON RANKE

Leopold von Ranke (1795–1886), titular professor of history in the University of Berlin from 1825 to 1871, was the acknowledged leader of the nineteenth-century scientific school of historians, whose banners were emblazoned with the Rankean cry of *wie es eigentlich gewesen:* "report the past as it actually happened." Ranke became so famous that in 1884, when he was elected the first honorary member of the American Historical Association, George Bancroft referred to him as "the greatest living historian." Ranke's first work came to the attention of the historical profession in 1824 with the publication of his *Histories of the Latin and Teuton Nations,* which enjoyed considerable professional success. Ranke's second book (from which the present selection is taken) on *The Ottoman and the Spanish Empires in the Sixteenth and Seventeenth Centuries* (1827), was based in part on a close reading of the unpublished *relazioni* (reports) of the Venetian ambassadors, which served as a policy guide for the Venetian Senate and as an invaluable source for latter-day historians. Part of Ranke's fame comes from the fact that he was the first European historian to make use of these reports.

I F an intelligent man pondered over the posture of the world in those days, what must he have expected of the son of such a father?

It was manifest that only a sovereign of liberal feelings, only one more disposed to gratify the world and to enjoy it than to dispose of it after his own views, and capable of allowing others a spontaneous course of action, would have been in a condition, if not to reconcile the discordant feelings of the nations, at least to soothe them, and prevent the outbreak of their passions. It was plain that the heir of the Spanish monarchy, destined to the sovereignty over such heterogeneous countries, had need of manners marked by dignified condescension and affability, and of a cheer-

ful temper to win the confidence of every individual. If this was undoubtedly to be wished, it might also perhaps have been expected. It might have been supposed that a sovereign, brought up under a sense of his great destiny, would have elevated his soul to a nobler view of things than such as is usually afforded by the narrowing influences of a meaner station. Reared in the feeling that he was the head of the nobility, should he not have sought to fashion his character to that cheerful, engaging chivalry, that sits so well on the young?

When Philip left Spain for the first time, and presented himself in other countries, the first thing remarked in him was the great external resemblance he bore to

From Leopold von Ranke, *The Ottoman and the Spanish Empires in the Sixteenth and Seventeenth Centuries,* trans. by Walter K. Kelly (London, 1843), pp. 42–47.

his father. There was the same white rather than pale visage, the same fair hair, the same chin and mouth. Neither was he tall; Philip was somewhat less in stature, more neatly made, and weaker than his father. The comparison was soon carried further. The son's features did not seem to indicate the acute penetration that characterized those of the father. It was perceived that Philip, far from vying with the latter in natural affability, was far surpassed by him in that respect. Whilst Charles was used, when escorted home by princes of the empire, to turn round, take off his hat, offer his hand to each and dismiss him with marks of amity, it was remarked with displeasure, that when the same attention was paid to Philip, he never once looked round him, but straight forward as he ascended the steps to his apartments. He took no delight in the chase, or in arms; he even declined the invitations of his father, preferring to remain at home, and to converse with his favourites. It is evident that he lacked all those qualities that engage the affections of the people: the Italians and the Flemings were not a little averse to him, the Germans decidedly so.

It seemed, however, on his second departure from Spain in 1554, as though he abjured his former haughty, repulsive bearing, as though he sought to resemble his father in his outward deportment, and had got rid of that foolish fancy of which he was accused, namely, that he the son of an emperor was more than his father, who was but the son of a king. He displayed more condescension and affability, gave audience readily, and returned satisfactory answers. But in reality there was no change in him. He took heed to himself, because he wished to please the English, over whom he desired to be king. He nevertheless retained that proud, isolated impassibility which the Spaniards call *sosiego*. Sympathy and frankness were no virtues of his; he did not even concern himself to display a bountiful character; he showed himself averse to all personal participation in war.

From the time he returned to Spain after the peace of 1559, he never quitted the peninsula again. Even there he abstained from traveling from place to place, as his father and the kings before him had done. He fixed his royal residence in the castle of Madrid, and only left it to pursue that dreary road, shadowed by no tree, enlivened by no brook, that led to the Escurial, which he built among small naked hills, in a stony valley, as a residence for monks of the order of San Geronimo, and as a sepulchre for his father; or to go in spring to Aranjuez, where indeed he accompanied the chase to the mountains, and condescended to alcaldes and monteros, but without asking them a word about anything else than their offices, or suffering them to speak of anything besides their business. "Every one," says Cabrera [*sic*], "was duly regarded according to his station." At times we find him in the woods about Segovia, and once in Lisbon; but with these exceptions always at home. At first he used to show himself there on popular holidays, afterwards he suffered himself to be seen only once or twice a year in a gallery leading from his residence to his chapel; and in his latter years he desisted even from this, and remained constantly shut up in his apartments. The habitual expression of his face and figure was that of imperturbable calmness, a gravity carried to the utmost pitch, and its effect was felt to be exceedingly depressing. Even practised and esteemed orators were put out when they stood before him, and he measured them as usual with his eyes from head to foot. "Compose yourself (Sosegaos)," he would then say to them. He used to smile slightly in replying to anyone.

Philip II lacked, as we see, the physical activity of his father. He was no friend to those constant journeys, those hurried excursions to all places, wherever the sovereign's presence seemed necessary. He agreed with those who had applauded Ferdinand the Catholic, because he had rather caused his foreign wars to be carried on, than directed them in person, and who called to mind that even the armies of Charles had been more successful under the command of Pescara and Leira than under his own. Philip carried on war, but he remained aloof from it. A stirring life makes the soul more open, freer, and warmer. If there was always a certain rigidity of temper observable in Philip, it might possibly have been owing to the want of this activity.

On the other hand, Philip inherited from his father a larger share of the latter's energy in the affairs of the cabinet. True he avoided, even here too, all immediate intercourse with others, and we neither find him negotiating in person, nor taking part in the sittings of the council of state. But we shall see how the machinery of his government was so arranged that all the affairs of his widespread empire tended to his table as to a common center. Every resolution of his council of any importance was laid before him on a sheet of paper, on the margin of which he noted his own views and emendations. The petitions and the letters addressed to him, the suggestions of his ministers, and the secret reports, were all laid before him in his closet. His business and his pleasure was to read them. Seated there sometimes assisted by a trusty secretary, but often quite alone, he governed the large portion of the world subject to his sway, and exercised a kind of inspection and control over the rest; there he set in motion the hidden machinery that moved a great portion of the public affairs of the age. His diligence in this occupation was indefatigable. We have letters written by him at midnight: we find him despatching the unpleasant affairs of Flanders at one of his country seats, whilst his carriage halted on his way to join the queen. If he had to be present at an entertainment, he fixed it for a day on which there was at least no regular post to send off. He did not make his short journeys even to the Escorial without taking his papers with him, and perusing them by the way. As Margaret of Parma and Granvella, though inhabiting the same palace, communed together more by letter than by word of mouth, so he too wrote innumerable notes to his confidential ministers: Antonio Perez had two chests full of such autographs. Thus he was beyond comparison the most fully employed man of business in the world. His attention to his finances was uninterrupted, and we find him at times more accurately informed respecting them than his presidents. He wished to know everything that concerned his dominions. He had materials collected for a general statistical account of Spain for his own use, six volumes of which work are still preserved in the Escorial. But he wished his information to extend even to particulars. He had correspondents in every diocese, who reported to him how the clergy and the holders of the benefices conducted themselves. He had always a prelate at each of the universities who acquainted him how the members of the colleges were versed in the sciences. Those who were candidates for any place he usually knew, even before they were presented, as well as though he had been personally acquainted with them: he was aware of their character and their peculiarities; and once, when they were speaking to him in praise of a certain person's learning and ability, he retorted. "You say nothing to me of his amours." Thus he ruled his dominions in peace; in turbulent times he redoubled his attention. It excited wonder to see, when the troubles broke out in Flanders, how accurately he was informed about all persons who might have had any leaning to the new opinions, how exactly he knew, not only their meetings, but also the age, appearance, character, and intercourse of each; and how, instead of receiving information from Margaret on these matters, he was, on the contrary, able to impart it to her. Now, it was just in the same manner he managed his foreign affairs. He had at all the leading courts, not only public ambassadors who sent him reports, or came to Spain to give him information by word of mouth, but he had also secret emissaries whose letters were addressed directly to himself. A historian might well cherish the wish that he might share with this king the comprehensive and thorough knowledge he possessed of his own times. Philip sat and read all these reports, and concentrated all their contents, and directed them to his own ends. He weighed them for himself. If he thought them good, he communicated them to one or other of his confidential ministers; if not, he buried them in perpetual silence. Thus he lived in complete solitude, and yet was personally acquainted, as it were, with the whole world; secluded from its contemplation, and yet its real governor; himself in almost motionless repose, and yet the originator of movements that affected all the world. Grown old and gray, weary and dim-sighted over his toils, he still did not give them up. His daughter, the infanta Isabella, who was moulded entirely after his own heart, for whom he had a cordial regard, and to whom he would go even at night, and communicate to her some welcome news, used to sit for three or four hours with him; and though he did not admit her into all his secrets, still she helped him to read the petitions and memorials of private persons, and to provide for the affairs of the home administration.

Now what was the aim of such incessant industry throughout his long life? Was it the welfare of the kingdoms of which he swayed the scepter? the prosperity of his subjects? This might have been supposed in the beginning of his reign, so long as he seemed to abjure his father's schemes, and his thirst for glory, and to look only to his own dominions. But he soon began to play a very busy part in the complicated affairs of Europe. Was it then his purpose, as it was perhaps in his power, to heal the wounds of his times? We cannot affirm either the one or the other. Obedience and the Catholic faith at home, the Catholic faith and subjection [to Spain abroad.] He was himself devoted, with monkish attachment, to the outward observances of the Catholic worship. He kissed the hand of a priest after mass, to show archdukes who visited him what reverence is due to such men. To a lady of rank, who stood upon the

steps of the altar, he said, "That is no place either for you or me." How diligently, with what care and expense, did he gather the sacred relics from all countries that had become Protestant, that such precious things might not be lost to Catholicism and Christendom. This was surely not from indwelling religion; yet a sort of indwelling religion, capable of swaying the moral character, had grown up in him, out of the conviction that he was born to uphold the external service of the Church, that he was the pillar of the Church, that such was his commission from God. If by this means he brought it to pass, that the majority of Spaniards, full of the like feelings, did, as an Italian says "not merely love, not merely reverence, but absolutely adore him, and deem his commands so sacred, that they could not be violated without offense to God;" at the same time, by a singular illusion (if indeed we are justified, in supposing his conduct to have sprung from an illusion of his own, and not to have been deliberately pursued to delude others), he came to regard the progress of his own power and the progress of religion as identified, and to behold the latter in the former. In this he was confirmed by the people of the Netherlands, who revolted simultaneously from him, and from the pope. In truth, the zeal that animated him was none other than that which had actuated Charles the Bold and Maximilian I, the zeal, namely of exalting the Burgundian and Habsburg house, which had become conjoined with religious purposes since the days of Charles V, only the union of these two motives was much stronger in him: and if he sought to conquer England, and to obtain the crown of France for his nephew and his daughter, it was with the full persuasion that he was acting for the best interests of the world, and for the weal of souls. If, on the one hand, his reserve and his gravity unfitted him for presiding over the nations he ruled with kindness, affability, and as a father; on the other hand, his narrow and fanatical constitution of mind placed it far beyond his power to become the reconciling spirit of his distracted times; he was, on the contrary, a great promoter and augmenter of the discord.

Two points are further to be remarked, with reference to his administration. The one, as regards his ministers; the other, as regards the means he employed to obtain his ends.

Whether it was from the compulsory pressure of his multitudinous businesses or that he was induced thereto by personal confidence, he left his ministers great freedom, and an open range of action. Espinosa was long called the monarch of Spain; Alva had his hands free in the Netherlands. We will look more minutely into the changes of his ministers, and their position. He seemed to be dependent on, and ruled by, many of his confidential advisers. Moreover, it was to no purpose anyone proffered a complaint against these men: his first answer was, that he relied on his advisers; and however often their accusers returned to the charge, they were always met with the same reply. People complained, that not only the interests of foreign powers, but those of the king himself, were betrayed and ruined through the private feelings and passions of these ministers. Now, it is very well worth noting his manner of dealing with them. To their best suggestions he seemed to lend but half an ear, and for a while it was as though they had said nothing; but at last, he put their ideas into operation, as though they had proceeded from himself. He used to say, that he stayed away from the council of state, in order that the passions of the several members might be free to display themselves the more unreservedly, and that if he had but a faithful reporter of all that passed, he could have no better means of information. But he went still farther than this. He suffered incensed enemies to pursue each other into his very cabinet, and he received the memorials of the one party against the other. As the close secrecy he observed on all things was notorious, no one scrupled to confide to him the most private matters,

and things that would never have been imparted to any other. Such communications did not always produce the full effect intended, but some of them did; and Philip was always filled with suspicion. Never was it easier for anyone than for him to withdraw his accustomed confidence, and to stint in his wonted favour. For a while he would conceal his secret displeasure. Perhaps the minister had important matters still in hand, perhaps his personal cooperation was necessary for the accomplishment of some purpose. So long as the case stood thus, he dealt with him warily as with a foreign power, and frequently, meanwhile, would neither comply with the minister's desires, nor absolutely reject them. But at last, his displeasure broke out all at once. Cabrera remarks of no few, that his disfavour was their death. So much may have been implied by the saying proverbial at his court, that it was not far from his smile to his dagger. The whole spirit of his favourites hung on his good will; without it, they sank into nothingness.

As he changed his ministers, so too he changed the measures they were to carry out, ever keeping his ends steadily in view. How numerous, and how various, were the courses he struck out in the affairs of Flanders alone. It is a mistake, to suppose he knew how to adopt no other devices than those of force. Undoubtedly he acquiesced in Alva's cruel measures, not however from cruelty, but for the sake of the result he expected. When this did not ensue, he selected Requesens for the express reason, that he was a moderate man, and commissioned him to employ milder means. He sent Don John, who was acceptable to the people of the Netherlands, because he appeared to be their countryman, with definite orders to conclude a peace. Failing in this, he again reverted to force. In this he may be compared to his great grandfather, Maximilian, who was continually adopting new means to arrive at his ends: only Maximilian broke off at an early stage of his proceedings, while Philip always pushed matters to the very utmost: Maximilian always seemed highly excited, Philip invariably maintained the most unruffled composure. Never did he give way to any impulse of temper. There never arrived a despatch from Flanders, however good or bad its news, that could produce the least change in his countenance. On receiving the first intelligence of the victory at Lepanto, the greatest that had been achieved by Christendom for 300 years, he said, "Don John risked a great deal," and not a word more. Upon the greatest mischance that could befall him, the loss of his fleet, on which he had exhausted the resources of Spain, on which he had built the grandest hopes, and which he had deemed invincible, he said, "I sent it out against men, and not against the billows"; and having said this, he seemed perfectly calm. The only gesticulation he was observed to make, when anything occurred quite contrary to his expectation, or when any word let fall provoked him very much, was that same one which is noticed in the gravest Arabs; he clutched his beard in his hand.

There are in this dismal life some spots of surpassing gloom. Why was his son Don Carlos disposed to rebel against him? It is now but too certain that he wished to do so. Assuredly the prince presented a decided contrast to his father; the latter, particularly at first, all calm and pacific; the former, on the contrary, fired with an enthusiastic love of arms, ardently attached to the soldiery, and of an impetuosity of character that disdained to conceal ambition, cruelty, or any other passion. He displayed a brilliant munificence, strikingly opposed to the king's frugality. The more restrictions there were imposed on him, the more passionate became his inclinations. He was still very young when the question began to be agitated of entrusting him with some lieutenancy. But this was not done. He had reason to expect a greater degree of independence from his marriage, which was already negotiated and agreed on; but the father took to himself the son's destined bride. As often as a war broke out he longed

to join in it, and he always was forced to remain at home. At last he made it the sole object of his wishes, that the pacification of the Netherlands should be committed to him: Alva was preferred to him. Thus this impetuous spirit, shut out on all sides from active exertion, and driven back upon itself, was thwarted and irritated to madness. Now would Carlos kill Alva, and escape by flight from his father; now had he no rest day or night, till he cried out that he meditated a deed against a man he hated, for which he besought absolution beforehand, till he was frantic enough to give the theologians of Atocha grounds for surmising that his father was the hated foe whose life he threatened. Did his father then leave him to pine away and die in prison? Or is the story really true, that the coffin in which Carlos lay was opened, and his head found severed from his body? Be it enough to say, that Philip lived on such deplorable terms with his son, that he must either fear everything at his hand, or doom him to death without pity.

This matter had no doubt some influence on the subsequent discipline practised by this monarch with his children. When he had his heir apparent, Philip, brought up for an unusual length of time, and with injurious severity among women, it was thought that he bore Don Carlos in mind. He took care not to give him a grandee for his tutor. He did not even suffer, as it is said, that his son and his faithful daughter, Isabella, should speak with each other unknown to himself.

He lived, however, to see the natural and inevitable result of all this. As his end drew nigh he saw his kingdom exhausted of men, and burdened with debts, his foes and his revolted subjects powerful, alert, and provided with means of attack; but the successor, who might have remedied those evils, and resisted those enemies, he saw not. His son was wholly incapable. It is said that this conviction once quite overcame him. He bewailed it to his son-in-law, Albert of Austria, and to Isabella, whom he greatly loved: "To his grace in bestowing on him

so great a realm, God had not been pleased
to add the grace of granting him a successor
capable of continuing to rule it. He com-
mended the realm to them both. The old
king said this with tears, he who had shed
no tears at the death of his children."

The Character of a King

CARL GEORG BRATLI

Carl Georg Bratli was a Danish historian, who, at the close of the nineteenth
century, became fascinated by the legends that had grown up around the
historical character of Philip II. In quest of the origins of the "black legend,"
Bratli visited the royal Spanish archives of Simancas outside Madrid, where he
gained an intimate knowledge of sixteenth-century documents, some of which
he reprints in his masterpiece, *Philip II, King of Spain*, originally published in
1909 in Danish and then translated into French and Spanish. The present selection, which was revised and augmented by the author, is taken from the French
edition of 1912.

AMONG the great figures of modern history, few have been the object of
so much investigation and less understood than the eldest son and successor of
Charles V. The reign of that prince, which
fills the whole of the second half of the
sixteenth century and which is so rich in
remarkable and highly important events,
has been studied . . . by the most competent European historians, whose persistent
and profound investigations have contributed greatly to our understanding of that
fascinating period of history.

The last half of the sixteenth century
presents the climax and at the same time
the cessation of a prolonged, stubborn, and
implacable struggle between two principles,
two politico-religious systems: liberty and
authority. It is Philip II who was summoned by destiny to personify authority
and absolutism during this whole period.
It is in his person that the idea of monarchical and religious unity was incarnated;
he was the symbol of unity not only for
Spain, but for all Spain's vast possessions,
and at the same time for the entire Roman
Catholic world. Everyone looked to him as
the chosen instrument for the maintenance
of the existing order of things, and as the
great defender of the faith in the war
against the shattering tendencies of the
Reformation.

It is not astonishing, then, that in his
lifetime, Philip was worshipped as an idol
by his subjects and coreligionists, but was
utterly detested by the partisans of the new
ideas of the Reformation.

In order to acquire exact and detailed
knowledge of this remarkable man, who
was honored by Pope Pius V with the title
of "the right hand of Christianity," and to
whom the Protestants gave such outrageous
names as "devil of the South," "Herod,"
and "Tiberius," one will first of all have to
observe him in his own household, study
his habits, examine the written documents
that he has left, and consider the memoirs
and the other works which discuss his life
and his work. In following his voluminous
correspondence, written in his own hand,

From Carl Georg Bratli, *Philippe II, roi d'Espagne* (Paris, 1912), pp. 13–15; 102–119; 127–129. Reprinted by permission of Librairie Honoré Champion. [Editor's Translation].

with his additional notes and corrections, one has testimony enough of his extraordinary love of work and his steadfast force of personality which was such a characteristic mark of his government. It is, in large part, thanks to these memoirs, that modern scholars have, quite frankly, arrived at a more favorable estimation of his character . . . than that left him by those historians for whom traditions, religious beliefs, and political prejudice count more than authentic documents.

We should begin with his relations with God, if we wish to describe the person and character of Philip II.

In popular opinion, this King is still judged as a type of bigot and hypocrite in the most abominable form. . . . Others have depicted him as an ambitious fanatic for whom religious ideas and institutions were only instruments in the service of purely secular and political projects. It is this interpretation that is usually given to his relations with the Inquisition.

However, Philip's piety which, for many people of that day, seemed to represent an exaggerated and morbid religiosity, must rather be considered as an expression of that very tendency towards mysticism which in the sixteenth century found such favorable soil in Spain and which produced such figures as Louis de Grenada (1504–1591). The same desire for a contemplative life, the same concern for the soul's salvation which led Charles [V] to Yuste, bound Philip to the Escorial, where, as a simple monk, he shared, as often as possible, in the friar's pious prayers. It was in the divine service, in prayer or in the nearly ecstatic state into which he often fell before a crucifix, an image of the Virgin, or of a saint that Philip sought and found the strength to shoulder the anxieties, misfortunes . . . and acute cares of government.

. . . Philip displayed a great respect for churches, convents, priests, and religious images. There is the story that when he met a priest carrying the image of Saint Viatic to a sick person, he joined the group and accompanied them to their destination. In 1596, paralyzed by gout, he was returning one day in his coach from his sister's, the Empress Dowager Maria, who lived in a convent in Madrid, when he encountered the holy sacrament being carried through the street. He asked his son Philip to assist him, and he descended from his coach and followed the priests, remarking that he would walk with them all the way himself if he could make better use of his legs.

We know also that Philip's respect for the clergy as representatives of God went so far that he never allowed a priest to kiss his hand.

Philip's personal piety was thus the source of the zeal that he showed for the care and welfare of the Church. We know the energetic efforts he employed to guide the work of the Council of Trent to its successful conclusion; also it was he who reestablished in Spain the provincial synods which had not been convoked since the time of Jimenez de Cisneros. He took special care to see that ecclesiastical posts were conferred on deserving and capable men. . . . On one point in particular, Philip proved himself intellectually superior to his age: [though deeply pious] he was not superstitious, and he was always contemptuous of the auguries and prophecies of astrologers.

[One legend concerning Philip's religious life needs further discussion.] There are the most fantastic versions current concerning Philip's relations to the Inquisition. These legends make him out as the founder of the institution and the inventor of the *auto-de-fé* [the ceremony in which the secular authorities punished, often by burning at the stake, persons condemned by the Inquisition]. But we now know that, while defending and seriously supporting the Inquisition, he was only following — on this point in particular — the instructions of his father. We must also recognize that that tribunal acted with a sincerity and humanity that was rather uncommon in those days; indeed, we have it on good authority that its procedure was superior to that of most secular tribunals. One can no longer attribute to Philip himself the efforts to introduce the Inquisition, in its Spanish form, into Naples, Milan, and Flanders. From a letter written by Philip to the Duke of Alba, in 1565, . . . Philip resolved that the Inquisition was not to be introduced into Naples. Alba had proposed to introduce the Inquisition in the Spanish form, but Philip wrote that such an action was never his intention and that Alba must adjust this question consistent with local practice.

People have likewise reproached Philip for introducing the Inquisition into the Spanish navy. But in reading the instructions that the inquisitor-general, Gaspar de Quiroga (d. 1594) sent to the newly-appointed maritime inquisitor, one gains, unquestionably, another impression of the supposed severity of that measure. In fact, the naval inquisitor's principal mission, it seems, was to watch over the soldiers and the galley oarsmen to see that they were well-treated and adequately provided for; he was to visit the poor and the sick to find out whether they were receiving enough to live on; and he was also to watch over the morals and the living conditions of the hospital attendants. . . .

[Linked to his pious nature, we find that] One of the most striking traits of Philip's character was his love of justice; he showed few personal preferences, and his implacable severity was directed without distinction against the great lord and the lowly serf, the rich and the poor. Often he showed an extreme harshness to the great nobles of his realm, who had drawn upon themselves the full brunt of his anger. . . .

Philip was a very good judge of men; and, if he had spoken to the person even once, it was rare he was deceived in his judgment. During audiences, he had the habit of looking at the person he received with such a fixed stare that it often happened that the person became so upset and nervous that the King was obliged to quiet him by a "Sosegaos" [a period of extreme quiet]. After that, he would generally listen to them with great patience and without interrupting them; his replies were always couched in the most polite and affable form.

In the field of secular government, Philip introduced a series of very urgent reforms. He abolished the practice, common until then, of the selling or arbitrary distribution of offices. After he had taken this step, no one could assume a public office without having obtained his university degree. Philip read with patience and extreme care all requirements of an office . . . , and, through his numerous secret agents, he then learned all about the capabilities and the personal qualifications of the candidates. . . .

But King Philip was not more exacting of his officials and servants than of himself: he, after all, accomplished, during a half century, a personal labor that we might well consider impossible if the quantities of documents did not constitute a testament traced by his own hand. The most ordinary and insignificant communications as well as the gravest affairs of state, captured his interest, and he wished always to examine and weigh them by himself. He responded to all these communications or provided [his secretaries] with minute and interminable remarks and corrections, which often, it is true, dealt only with usage and spelling. It is interesting to recall that he loved this paperwork and often said, if he had been a private citizen, he would be a rich man. One can estimate . . . that Philip spent daily 8 or 9 hours with pen in hand. While traveling, when he could not write, he generally carried books and documents which he could read on the trip.

After his interests in the Church and the State, it was art that Philip liked best; we can call him the Maecenes of his age. He possessed a quite impressive knowledge of architecture and of the plastic arts; and his critical sense rested on profound study. Although one cannot point to a painting or a piece of sculpture that can be attributed to Philip himself; we can be certain that he executed personally a great number of designs for monuments and for their interior decoration. . . .

Since the time of Philip the Good (1396–1467), it was the tradition in the Burgundian court to attach hired artists to the prince's service. . . . It was in "La Casa del Tersoro," which happened to communicate directly with the palace in Madrid, where the king installed his artists, a many-hued troop of the leading celebrities of the time. Philip could scarcely have been a more ardent patron nor a more sincere friend to these painters, sculptors, and architects whom he rewarded generously and with whom he associated with greater familiarity than with the grandees of Spain itself.

Philip's interest in the sciences was nearly as ardent as that in the plastic arts. Always . . . full of zeal for reforms, he intervened personally in all the fields of Spanish intellectual life. With his sense of order and exactitude, he laid the foundation for one of Europe's greatest and precious scientific collections. . . .

Moreover, a vast number of universities, colleges, seminaries, and schools owed their creation or reorganization to Philip. We will not enter into the details . . . suffice it to note that his role has not been sufficiently appreciated by non-Spanish authors, whose attention has been drawn too often to the economic decline of the country during the last ten years of the [sixteenth] century. . . .

[In summary we can say that] Philip should be judged differently as a man and as a King. We have seen that all those who had the least personal contact with him had only praise for him; [certainly] he possessed rare and captivating qualities. He was naturally modest, reserved, even timid, and he preferred solitude and the life of the mind to participation in rough and tumble politics. . . . The apparent patience and calm with which he received all bad news and suffered all his misfortunes was only the result of a violent effort of the will. In the last years of his life he would often fall ill after receiving word of new defeats.

But the care and slowness with which he examined everything, coupled with his ir-

resolution on important matters of state . . . were the cause of great delays, which assured his enemies a considerable advantage.

Another of Philip's important character traits was his pessimism which, from his youth, inspired in him a defiance toward the world. He always wanted to inspect and check over the most insignificant as well as the most important affairs. Certainly the care and the tenacity with which he conformed to the rules which he himself had outlined, . . . his political good sense, and his keen attention to matters of state . . . most justify the title "El Prudente" — The Prudent.

Without a doubt, there has scarcely been a sovereign who has felt the responsibility and the vapidness of royalty to the same degree as Philip II. When, in the course of years, he saw many of his plans and grandiose dreams vanish; when misfortunes, ordeals, and humiliations flooded over him, he found the strength to endure them through the certainty that he was fighting for loftier interests than those connected with this world: . . . "God is my witness," he wrote to members of the Cortes on the occasion of the expedition against England in 1588, "that it was not the desire to gain new kingdoms that guided me, but the zeal for His service and the hope of glorifying the Holy Faith: for this I have risked everything: my patrimony, the cause of God, the glory of the State, and my own honor."

From the vantage point of the twentieth century, we may say that this "fanaticism" of Philip's should really be called religious zeal; his "despotism," dynamic willpower; and his "cruelty," a justice that knew neither kin nor rank. But he himself became the martyr to his own high ideal. In a time when the political and religious evolution of Europe led into new paths . . . Philip was looked upon as an opponent of both the religious and social orders.

In the history of most countries, you come across rulers who have been, in the most striking manner, the expression of the national spirit; who have had a particular importance for the development of the State and who, for that reason, have been called national kings and queens. In modern times, one can cite as archtypes of these rulers: . . . Elizabeth of England, Henry IV of France, Christian IV of Denmark, Gustavus Vasa of Sweden, and Philip II of Spain.

We have seen previously that Philip possessed all the qualities that the Spanish national character appreciated and respected. We know that the Spanish had a very high ideal of royal dignity, an ideal which appears to be logically connected with the personal pride peculiar to that people. For his own part, the king was so conscious of his dignity and his responsibility that he secluded himself from his own people. However, he was by no means unapproachable. He observed faithfully one of his own rules made in 1543 which prescribed that he give audience to everyone regardless of rank; nevertheless, he only rarely made a public appearance, particularly during the last years of his reign.

To his way of thinking, the duties of a sovereign consisted above all in governing, that is to say, in working for his people and keeping a close check on the daily operations of the state's administrative offices.

Philip did not enjoy what we would today call, vulgarly, popularity. . . . His subjects admired, esteemed, and even loved him; but it was in a distant and impersonal way. Yet, under Philip II, every Spaniard knew that . . . no matter how great or how small the question at hand, it had always . . . been carefully weighed; indeed, Philip's brain seemed to encompass the whole dominion of human activity with a type of encyclopedic grasp. And the people had confidence in a King who made no distinction between his personal fate and that of his country, especially when it was a question of the defense and the conservation of their two most precious concepts: religion and the state. Such a King was after their own hearts.

People have asserted that Philip must bear a great deal of the responsibility for the decline that his country suffered at the end of his reign and which continued under his successors. We believe we have shown, however, that this decline had already started under Charles V. . . . We think, moreover, that we can prove that during a whole generation Philip succeeded in stopping this decline by sheer willpower and by the enormous work he shouldered himself.

If Philip had worked exclusively for material and worldly ends, he might well have become disheartened at the end of his career. But the struggle for his ideal and the unconquerable conviction that he had fought for higher goals rendered him indomitable in the face of his misfortunes. This is why history should list this steadfastness of purpose — which people so often term intolerance and fanaticism — as the most striking quality of that king.

The Prudent King

ROGER B. MERRIMAN

Roger Bigelow Merriman (1876–1945), educated at Harvard and Oxford Universities, joined the instructoral staff at Harvard in 1902, where in 1918 he became a full professor and in 1929 Guerney Professor of History and Political Science. In addition to his teaching duties at Harvard, Merriman assumed in 1931 the arduous tasks of House Master of Eliot House. Merriman began his research career as an historian of Tudor England but turned his attention to Spanish history soon after his arrival at Harvard. Seeing the need for a comprehensive history of the Spanish Empire, he ultimately made this his life's work. In a painstaking, workmanlike fashion he produced a massive four-volume history entitled *The Rise of the Spanish Empire*, the first volume being published in 1918, the last in 1934. Merriman was a careful craftsman, a follower of the Germanic schools of the nineteenth century, who adhered to the Rankean dictum "report the past as it actually happened." Although spartan in its literary tone, his works stand as a monument of historical labor, deservedly ranked with the works of William Hickling Prescott and Henry Charles Lea as the most graphic descriptions of Spain yet produced in the United States.

THE transition in Spanish history from Charles V to Philip II forms the antithesis to that from the Catholic Kings to the Emperor. In 1516 the destinies of the Spanish Empire had passed from native to alien hands; Spanish interests had been suddenly subordinated to those of the house of Hapsburg. Forty years later the reaction is complete; a process whose beginnings we have already noted in the Emperor's closing years has now attained its final stage; the outlook of the Spanish monarchy is once more thoroughly Hispanicized. The second of these transitions was more gradual than the first, but when it was completed it was much more permanent and far-reaching. Philip the Prudent will go down in history, both within the Iberian peninsula and without it, as the typical Spanish sovereign of all time.

So Spain at last got back her king. The wish, so often expressed by the Cortes of Charles V, that the Spanish monarch would stop his travelling, had now been fulfilled with the advent of his son. In all the thirty-nine years of life that remained to him Philip never once set foot outside the peninsula; and his constant presence there during so long a period, and in such a monarchical age, made its administration the faithful mirror of his own policy and ideals. Seldom in history has it been given to any sovereign to stamp the impress of his personality so deeply upon the lives of his subjects. If one would learn the destinies of the vast dominions over which he bore sway, one must begin with a careful study of his character and mentality; and these in turn cannot be adequately understood without remembering the Spanish origin and background out of which they were evolved. If Spain and the Spanish Empire were represented in Philip, so Philip was a typical product of Spain and the Spanish Empire.

His ancestry, of course, was predominantly Iberian. His father was half Spanish, his mother half Spanish and half Por-

From Roger Bigelow Merriman, *The Rise of the Spanish Empire in the Old World and the New,* 4 vols. (New York, 1918–1934), IV, pp. 3 and 18–40. Reprinted by permission of the Estate of Roger Bigelow Merriman.

tuguese; and she doubtless impressed him in his boyhood years with the idea that it was Portugal's destiny to be ultimately re-united with Spain, the idea which her own marriage with the Emperor had represented, and which Philip was subsequently, if only temporarily, to carry out. The influence of the Empress was also a potent cause of Philip's proverbial respect for the clergy. She was very devout and spent many hours in prayer; from his infancy the prince was surrounded by clerics and subjected to ecclesiastical influences. The other two chief things that stand out, as one reads the story of his early years, are the joylessness of his life and the deficiencies of his linguistic equipment. He was never allowed to have a playmate worthy of the name; the Portuguese Ruy Gómez da Silva, who afterwards became his chief councillor, was perhaps the nearest to it, but Ruy Gómez was Philip's senior by no less than five years. The Empress insisted that the prince be treated with the respect due to "the son of the greatest emperor that the Christian world had ever seen"; his every movement was regulated by an etiquette so strict that it was scarcely possible for him to laugh. Everything combined to make him cold and reserved, to train him to conceal his real feelings, to enhance the characteristics of gravity and melancholy which he had inherited from his father. The latter, though absent from Spain during the greater part of his son's early life, had given much thought to the question of the prince's studies, and had provided him with the best tutors that could be had. Philip made good progress in science and in art; he read much history, and gave promise at an early age of possessing unusually sound political judgment. But for languages he showed even less aptitude than the Emperor; indeed it was well said of him that from his childhood days he preferred to communicate by writing rather than by word of mouth. Even in his native Castilian he always spoke slowly, though with great precision, and he seemed to have much difficulty in choosing his words. He

could write and speak his Latin reasonably well. He could understand a little French and Italian, and speak a little French; but to converse readily in these or any other foreign tongues was utterly beyond him. Small wonder that he was so uncosmopolitan. He had no means of free communication with any one beyond the Pyrenees.

Numerous contemporaneous accounts of his physical traits have come down to us; those of the Venetian ambassadors are on the whole the most valuable, though we have Spanish, French, and English testimony besides. Philip was of less than medium stature, but finely proportioned, and of a carriage "so straight and upright as he loseth no inch in height"; the grace and dignity of his presence were further enhanced by the care, restraint, and elegance with which he dressed. His eyes were blue and his hair and beard light, so that he seemed at first sight to be rather a Fleming than a Spaniard. His large protruding under-jaw and lip, though considerably less prominent than those of his father, were yet sufficiently noticeable to betray the Hapsburg ancestry. In early manhood he wore his beard "short and pointed, after the Spanish fashion"; later in life he permitted it to increase in length and breadth until it approached the style customary in the Netherlands. The pallor of his complexion was also remarked on by all observers, and most of them drew the proper conclusion, namely, that it indicated a weak stomach and lack of exercise. Reddened eyes were a penalty of his excessive devotion to the written word both day and night. He ate slowly, sparingly, and usually alone, restricting himself to meats and the "most nutritious foods"; almost all the accounts of him emphasize his avoidance of fruits and of fish. He also suffered from asthma, stone, and gout; and though his doctors recommended him to go hunting and get out into the open air "as the best means of strengthening his body and distracting his mind from melancholy reflections," he paid little or no attention to them; apparently, too, he was haunted by the fear lest he should die as the result of an accident, and kept constantly before his mind the experience of the king of France. He was totally deficient in that capacity for sudden and almost superhuman physical exertion which, in the case of some of Spain's greatest empire builders, alternated so strikingly with long periods of doing nothing at all; "Ohne Hast, aber ohne Rast" is an accurate description of him, if one remembers that his activities were not those of the body, but of the mind. He was ever a great sleeper, and the tendency increased with advancing years. In the later part of his life he seldom rose before half past nine, and always took a long nap after his mid-day meal; sometimes, it is true, he would work till midnight, but more often he retired early in the evening to read for a couple of hours before he closed his eyes; indeed it was well said of him when he was an old man that his only recreation was repose. The effect of these habits on his policy and methods of government was foreseen with striking clarity by the Venetian ambassador in 1559. "From them it results," so remarks the report, "that though he is at the age of youthful appetites and insatiable desire to rule, nevertheless all the actions of his Majesty are invariably directed, not to the aggrandizement of his kingdoms by war, but rather to their conservation through peace." The counsels of the Emperor to avoid aggressive action and rest on the defensive had certainly been heard by willing ears. What his father had acquired with the sword, Philip proposed to preserve with the pen. From first to last he was the "Prudent King."

Reading and writing occupied the major portion of Philip's day; indeed he not seldom continued to read and to write while taking a drive in his carriage. We have already alluded to his preference for written over oral communications; add to this his firm determination to keep in touch with everything that was going on, even in the remotest corner of his vast dominions, and his own persistent unwillingness to leave the centre of Castile, and it furnishes the key to his methods of government. He had the highest possible sense of his royal prerogatives and duties; he had taken deeply to heart his father's injunction to direct everything himself, and never to give his full confidence even to the most faithful of his ministers, and the natural result was that his time was completely occupied with receiving and answering reports and letters. Most of these were concerned with immediate affairs of state, and their number mounted so fast that in 1566 Philip took the first measures for their conservation in the ancient castle of Simancas, which soon became a national archive. Others — like the famous *Relaciones Topográficas* — were elaborate answers to royal requests for information in regard to existing conditions from all the cities of the realm. "They are sent to him," writes the Venetian ambassador Morosini, "from all sorts and conditions of men and treat of every sort and kind of subject, both great and small, in such fashion that it may be said that the number of them is infinite; indeed, having so many subjects and trusting no one, and insisting that everything pass under his own hand and eye, he is so perpetually preoccupied with this business, with so great labor and toil, that I have heard many people say that they would not for the world be the ruler of so many states as is his Majesty, if it meant living the kind of life he lives." Reports, reports, and ever more reports; Philip was literally submerged with them in his later years, and moreover he did not stop at reading them; he annotated them, as he went along, with comments on matters as absurdly trifling as the spelling and style of the men who had written them — all in that strange, sprawling hand of his, one of the most illegible hands of an age more than usually replete with chirographical difficulties. A story of somewhat uncertain origin which has come down to us, in regard to the results of a night's work of this sort, is perhaps worth quoting in this connection; it is primarily a proof of Philip's unlimited patience and self-control, but it also reveals his great kindness to his servants, an excellent test of a gentleman. Apparently the king had sat up unusually late, covering sheet after sheet with handwriting and annotations; when at last he had finished, he called his attendant to throw sand over the papers in order to dry the ink. The attendant, however, was so confused and appalled by the responsibility placed on his shoulders that instead of the sand box, he took up the ink pot and emptied its contents over his Majesty's labors; but Philip forbore to reproach him. "*This* is the sand, *that* is the ink," was his only comment on the damage that had been done.

If we can visualize Philip niggling over these innumerable reports, we are furnished with the explanation of much else besides. He possessed a tenacious memory, and was resolved to superintend everything himself; "bien es myrar á todo" is a phrase frequently found in his writings. But he was curiously unable to separate the essentials from the details, or to persuade himself ever to delegate the latter to subordinates; he was like the historian who has vastly more material than he can possibly hope to handle. And the obvious result was that under his rule the administration of the Spanish Empire became more notorious than ever for its slowness. It had been bad enough under the Emperor, but it was to be infinitely worse under his son. So poor were the means of communication in those days, so vast and so widely scattered were the dominions over which Philip ruled, that the only possible method of governing them successfully was to invest the king's local representatives with a large measure of independence. But this was just what Philip could never bring himself to do; and he was the more convinced that his own way was the only right one because it tallied so closely with the precepts of his imperial father. It was centralization carried to the breaking point, pushed so far that it paralyzed efficiency. While Philip was deciding how the sailors on the Armada could best be kept from swearing, Sir Francis Drake raided the Spanish coast. His viceroys and ambassadors, who were constantly kept waiting for orders, and for subsidies to enable them to carry them out, frequently expressed the hope that death would come to them by way of Spain, for thus they would be certain to live to a ripe old age. Prescott prints part of a letter addressed to Philip by Luis Manrique, the grand almoner, telling him in vigorous terms of the discontent of his subjects because of his manner of doing business, "sitting forever over your papers, from your desire, as they intimate, to seclude yourself from the world, and from a want of confidence in your ministers. Hence such interminable delays as fill the soul of every suitor with despair. . . . God did not send your Majesty and all the other kings, his viceroys on earth, to waste their time in reading or writing, nor yet in meditation and prayer." The Cortes also pointedly advised him to relieve himself of the details of administration and intrust them to the councils and tribunals to which they belonged, so that business might be transacted more speedily and his time be free for weighty affairs of state and war. And the tragedy of it all was that these disastrous mistakes were really brought about chiefly as a result of one of Philip's finest qualities, his exalted idea of the duties of kingship. Certainly his worst enemies cannot justly accuse him of being a *roi fainéant*.

Two other outstanding virtues of Philip call for special comment; they were both of them salient characteristics of his great-grandmother, Isabella the Catholic, and in both he showed notable improvement over the ways of his father. The first was his love of justice and determination to see it done throughout his dominions. "Justice is his favorite interest," writes the Venetian ambassador in 1563; "and in so far as its administration concerns him, he does his duty well." "He is by nature the justest of rulers," writes another in 1584, "and his justice extends so far that were it not regulated by the greatest prudence and experience in the affairs of the world, it would pass into severity." The good old custom of the Catholic Kings — that of hearing the pleas of their subjects on Fridays — had by this time fallen into desuetude, and Philip made no effort to revive it; in this matter at least — and it would seem to be the exception that proves the rule — the king consented to delegate to others; and it should be added that the judges whom he selected were famed for their probity and competence. Nevertheless, Philip was by no means entirely inaccessible, much as he loved solitude and detested the fatigue of audiences. We are assured that on the way to and from divine service, "he accepted all the supplications that were handed to him, and that if any one desired to speak with him, he stopped courteously to listen"; but Philip never showed, either by expression or gesture, how he proposed to deal with such requests; they were all distributed to the officials whom they respectively concerned, to be acted upon favorably or the reverse as the case might be; if favorably the signature of the king was necessary before final action could be taken.

The other matter by which Philip earned the gratitude and respect of his subjects was his gradual restoration of the pristine simplicity of the royal court and household. It will be remembered that in the days of Charles V there had been constant complaints of the luxurious "Burgundian" fashions of the imperial establishment, and demands for a return to the ancient customs of Castile; and at the beginning of Philip's reign there was no evidence of improvement. When he got back from the Netherlands his establishment was fully as magnificent as ever it had been in the days of his father; it numbered no less than 1500 persons, of whom nine-tenths were Spaniards, and the rest Flemings, Burgundians, Englishmen, Italians, and Germans; there are, moreover, countless testimonies to the excessive liberality of his grants and pensions, especially to Spaniards. But Philip himself was by nature frugal; the lavish cost of his household at the beginning of his reign represents rather the system which he had inherited from his father than what he would have chosen for himself; and as

the years went on, with his resources growing gradually smaller and smaller, with Spanish influence increasing and Burgundian growing correspondingly less, and with his own fondness for solitude becoming steadily more marked, his natural frugality began to assert itself. In the middle of his reign we have numerous evidences that the expenses of the royal household diminished year by year; at Madrid only barely enough pomp and circumstance were maintained to suffice for the preservation of the dignity of a king. And at the end, we find Philip living and dying in a little cell in the Escorial, only twelve feet square, unadorned and austere; it has been well said that the humblest monk of San Lorenzo "had a better room and better furnished than did the king of Spain." And the contrast, striking as it is with the ways of his father, is even more obvious with those of his son. The gorgeousness of the courts of Philip III and Philip IV was a prominent part of that great game of bluff behind which the internal rottenness of seventeenth-century Spain was concealed from the observation of foreigners; but the Prudent King's mode of living at the end of his days was an accurate mirror of existing national conditions. There can be no doubt that his subjects respected and admired him for it. If he had impoverished them, he had not done it for his own advantage.

Yet it would be a grave error to think of Philip as being naturally dead to all the pleasanter sides of life, and an even graver one to conceive of him as deficient in affection or incapable of friendship. The joylessness of his early years, to which we have already alluded, was but the inevitable consequence of the way in which he had been brought up; that he so loved to be alone during his later life was chiefly the result of circumstances and of a long series of family bereavements. Though he detested physical exercise of every sort, he got recreation in other ways. To the end of his life he took much pleasure in the jokes of professional buffoons — a peculiarly Spanish trait; we also get a glimpse of him playing piquet after dinner. Still more notable were his knowledge and enthusiasm for art. He loved music and could play the guitar; he was a patron of artists and a real connoisseur of painting and tapestry, sculpture, and architecture; we shall return to this phase of his activities in more detail in connection with the building of the Escorial. And there can be no doubt that in his earlier years he had various mistresses. The Venetian ambassadors and others frequently advert to his incontinence, but save for his liaison with the Princess of Eboli, about which there are so many divergent opinions, his amours do not seem to have had the slightest influence on his policy or methods of government; *si non caste, saltem caute.* But it was not, after all, in the company of his mistresses that Philip found his principal relaxation from the cares of state; indeed his ill health gives good reason for believing that he was rather less than more amorous than the average man. It was in the bosom of his own family that the king hoped to find the affection and companionship for which he hungered, and it was perhaps the deepest tragedy of his whole life that that hope, save for a few brief intervals, was destined to be disappointed.

His mother had died when he was but twelve years old; his first wife, Maria of Portugal, when he was eighteen, in bearing him the Infante Don Carlos. He wedded Mary Tudor at twenty-seven, but of the four years and four months during which he was married to her he passed less than one-third in England with the queen; the union had been dictated solely by political expediency; no child was born of it, and it was profoundly distasteful to Philip. Until the time of his return to Spain in 1559 he had scarcely tasted of the joys of a happy family life. Thereafter followed the brightest period of his whole existence. His third spouse, Elizabeth of Valois, reached Spain in the following January; her advent was the occasion of festivals and rejoicing, for it was regarded as the sign and seal of per-

manent reconciliation with France, and the new queen was popularly known as the *Reina de la paz*. Soon after her arrival she was stricken with smallpox; it was a light case, and she soon recovered, but it is interesting to read of the worries of her mother Catherine d' Medici, lest the disease should so disfigure her that she would lose her influence on her husband and imperil the safety of the Franco-Spanish understanding. Much depended indeed on whether or not the new queen should bear a child, and that question was not answered in the affirmative till six years after her arrival. On August 12, 1566, she was delivered of a daughter; the birth of the child was believed by the queen to have been due to the beneficent influence of the Spanish Saint Eugenius, whose remains the king, after interminable correspondence, had recently succeeded in having transferred to Toledo from their former resting place at St. Denis, and the Infanta was accordingly named Isabella Clara Eugenia. This daughter and her younger sister Catherine, born October 9, 1567, were the joy of their father's heart; and his affection for them increased with the death, on October 3, 1568, of their mother, who was mourned by the Spaniards as "the best queen that they had had or could have." That year, 1568, which also witnessed the death of Don Carlos, was unquestionably one of the saddest in Philip's whole life. But the necessity for a male heir took the precedence over everything else; in November, 1570, Philip married his fourth and last wife, Anne of Austria, the daughter of his cousin, the Emperor Maximilian II. She bore him four sons and one daughter, and died October 25, 1580, but of her children only one, who was to succeed his father as Philip III, lived to be more than eight years old. The Escorial was scarcely finished before it was filled with coffins. Philip had laid no less than seventeen members of his own family to rest there before he had completed his sixtieth year.

This terrible series of family bereavements is an element too often forgotten by those who have attempted to portray the life and character of Philip II. One chief reason why it has been so much neglected is doubtless the king's own extraordinary self-control. It was one of his fundamental principles that a sovereign should never, under any circumstances, exhibit his inmost feelings. "He is an adept at concealing his affections," writes Morosini in 1581. "No display of sorrow," was his order at the time of the death of the Infante Don Ferdinand, in October, 1578; "nothing but processions and public prayer, returning thanks to God and humbly supplicating that he mitigate his wrath." Certainly it would be unfair to judge Philip by externals. But there has fortunately been preserved to us one glimpse of the man, as he really was in the bosom of his own family, one rift in the clouds of his impenetrable reserve; and that is a series of letters exchanged between him and his daughters Isabella and Catherine when he was absent on the campaign for the annexation of Portugal. These letters were discovered by Gachard in the archives of Turin, and published by him at Paris in 1884; they prove, beyond the possibility of doubt, that whatever the crimes and barbarities of which Philip may have been guilty in his capacity of Spanish monarch, he was a most loving and tender father, who longed, in his self-imposed isolation, for the sympathy and love which only a family can afford. Their contents are well-known and need not be repeated here: the evidences of his solicitude for his daughters' spiritual and physical welfare, his interest in the most intimate details of their daily life, his desire to know if they had begun to make use of the new Gregorian calendar, which went into effect during the period of the correspondence, his descriptions of the storms, the birds, the flowers, and of the local customs of his new kingdom, of everything, in fact, that would interest and amuse them. These letters also afford additional evidence of the king's friendly relations with his servants; his kindly tolerance of the cranky eccentricities of Madalena, the old nurse of the Infantas, forms the most amazing contrast to the cold, stern lord of the Spanish Empire, as portrayed by his official visitors. And yet it was the real man that these letters reveal — the man whom Philip was irrevocably determined that the outer world should never know.

It is not impossible that this contrast between the real and the official Philip, coupled with his firm resolve that the feelings of the former should never interfere with the duties of the latter, may point the way to the most reasonable solution of the mysteries that still surround the life and death of the son of his first marriage, the Infante Don Carlos, born July 8, 1545. For over three centuries and a half it has been a favorite theme of historians, novelists, and playwrights. All sorts of different theories have been offered in the explanation of it, but none of them has as yet been accorded any general acceptance. The legend which forms the basis of Schiller's famous tragedy, namely, that the Infante was sacrificed because of his love for his stepmother, Elizabeth of Valois, is devoid of any solid historical foundation; the tales that the sources of the trouble were his fondness for the Protestants, intrigues in the Netherlands, or deep-laid conspiracies against the royal authority in Spain, seem also, on the whole, to be unworthy of credence. On the other hand it would appear reasonably certain, despite the arguments of a recent authority to the contrary, that Don Carlos, from his earliest years, showed himself physically and mentally quite unfit for the vast responsibilities that would devolve upon him should he ever be permitted to succeed his father as the ruler of the Spanish Empire. His excesses in eating and in drinking, his passion for swallowing things and making others swallow them, his whimsical cruelties all tell the same tale; his picture by Sánchez Coello confirms it, as do the reports of the different ambassadors at the court of Madrid. These bad symptoms, sufficiently alarming during his boyhood, became rapidly worse when, at the age of sixteen, he "fell down a pair of stairs, broke his head and had two fits of an ague." It seems probable that his life was only saved on this occasion through the efforts of the learned Vesalius, who performed the operation of trepanning; and the measure of Philip's superstition and ignorance is revealed by the fact that he insisted on attributing his son's survival to the miraculous healing powers of the corpse of the cook of a Franciscan convent, long since dead, which was placed in bed beside the fever-stricken body of the Infante. In any case the evidences that Don Carlos would make an absolutely unendurable sovereign multiplied apace after his recovery from this accident. When his father, in the hope that the possession of authority might rouse him to some sense of his duties and responsibilities, tried the experiment of placing him in the Council of State, the Infante upset everything. He insulted and even assaulted his fellow councillors as no sane man would have done, and seemed to take a malicious pleasure in revealing the most important state secrets with which he had been intrusted. Irritated by the strictness of the surveillance to which he was subjected, he laid plans to flee to Italy or Germany and make trouble for his father abroad. Whether he had thoughts of murdering Philip seems much more doubtful. The difficulty, in this case, is not the lack of evidence, for there is an abundance of it, but rather to know how much to believe.

How to deal with the situation was a truly terrible problem — one of the most agonizing with which a royal father has ever been confronted; but early in the year 1568, Philip came to a decision. He was convinced that a strong monarchy was essential to the welfare of Spain. The experience of his predecessors had inspired him with a deep dread of the grandees, who had always seized the government when the kingship was weak; only a century before, under Henry the Impotent, there had been a striking demonstration of it, and Philip knew his Spanish history. Don Carlos promised to be far worse than Henry the Impotent had ever been; was it

not obvious, then, that Philip's duty to the state, of which he had the very highest conception, demanded that he should spare his realms from the perils of the rule of a madman? To imagine that he could answer this question in the affirmative without a pang is to ignore the evidence we have already adduced to prove that Philip had an intense family feeling and a deep affection for his own offspring; moreover, there were some risks in setting the Infante aside, for the king, in that moment, had no other son. It must have been a heart-rending decision to make, but finally, on the night of January 18, 1568, Philip summoned to his palace at Madrid Ruy Gómez, Luis de Quijada, and the Prior Antonio, and, "speaking as no man had ever spoken before," apprised them of the resolution he had taken. Then, with his helmet on his head and his sword in his hand, he led the way silently along the dark corridors of the palace to the apartments of the Infante. Everything had been carefully arranged beforehand. The bolts had been removed, and the door was opened without the least difficulty; before Don Carlos had waked up, the loaded pistols which he always kept by his bedside were taken away. The brief agonized queries of the Infante as to the meaning of it all were answered coldly and noncommittally by the king. The doors and windows were swiftly nailed up, Philip superintending the whole process with the utmost care. When all was finished he committed his son to the guard of the Duke of Feria, commanded that no one should be permitted to speak to him or bring him letters, and went out without speaking a word to the Infante. He was never to see him again.

Six months later, on July 24, the world learned that Don Carlos was no longer living, and stories were circulated for more than a century afterwards to the effect that the king had given orders that in one way or another he should be put to death. Some maintained that he was beheaded, and two of the various post-mortem examinations of the body (the last in 1812) appear to support this conclusion; but the evidences to the contrary are stronger and more reliable. The reports that he was strangled by slaves or suffocated in bed are totally lacking in solid historical foundation; while the tale that he was poisoned rests principally on the testimony of Antonio Pérez, who, at the time that he wrote his account, was bent on vilifying the name of Philip II. No one of the countless stories of the Infante's being made away with at the royal command can be definitely substantiated; that being the case, the king should be given the benefit of the doubt, if any continues to exist. Perhaps the best of all reasons for believing Philip to be innocent of the crime with which, before the days of critical historical scholarship, he was so often charged, is that it was unnecessary to the attainment of his ends; for he must have foreseen that Don Carlos's physical excesses in solitary confinement would be ultimately certain to cause his death. Philip's object was to remove his son from the possibility of any active participation in the life of the world, and he effected that end by imprisoning him. That the Infante's death, six months after his arrest, relieved the king from a most painful and embarrassing predicament is indubitable, but there is no adequate ground for believing that Philip was guilty of accelerating it.

The most recent authority on this tragic affair regards it simply as "a matter between father and son." He rejects the hypotheses of treasonable or heretical conspiracies on the part of the Infante, but fully admits his unfitness to rule; on the other hand he is very harsh in his verdict on the king. Philip's refusal to visit his son during his imprisonment seems to him utterly heartless. He cannot understand why the king failed to reward the improvement in Don Carlos's disposition toward him, which apparently took place after the Infante had been permitted to receive the communion at Eastertide, with any relaxation of the rigor of his confinement; he even blames Philip for his unwillingness to take part in the prince's funeral, which the king watched, with his accustomed calmness, from a window in the palace. But these strictures seem to reveal a very imperfect comprehension of the true character of Philip II. If the king was notoriously slow in making up his mind, he was equally firm in adhering to a course of action, once he had embarked upon it; to reverse the line of conduct which it had cost him such sorrow to adopt was unthinkable. Moreover, is not Philip's refusal to visit his son in his prison and to participate in his funeral quite as explainable on the hypothesis that he could not stand the strain upon his own affections as on that of heartless cruelty? We have seen that it was a cardinal principle of the Prudent King never to reveal his inmost feelings. How can we be sure that his heart was not filled with mortal anguish all the time — an anguish which he dreaded every moment to find himself unable to control?

Philip II as a Man and Statesman

REGINALD TREVOR DAVIES

Reginald Trevor Davies (1891–1953) was trained as a theologian, yet his tastes and attitudes were more historical than theological. Unlike Cecil John Cadoux, who attacked the relativistic approach towards history, Davies was sympathetic and emphatic. Described as a man of "unruffled good humor, serene equanimity, and gift of sympathy," he demonstrated these traits in his work. Oxford-trained, he spent almost his entire life at the college, where at the time of his death he was Dean of Degrees and Tutor in History to the non-collegiate Saint Catherine's Society. Davies was a familiar figure at the Bodelian Library, where he investigated his favorite topics — witchcraft and modern Spanish history. His two works on the Golden Age and decline of Spain have virtually become classics. Davies is particularly sympathetic to Philip II, and attempts to view the Spanish king within the framework of the values and environment of the sixteenth century.

HOWEVER much posterity has depreciated him, to his contemporaries Philip II appeared to "bestride the narrow world like a Colossus." His territories in Europe alone included not only the Spanish kingdoms, the Netherlands, Franche Comté, Sardinia, Sicily, and the Balearic Isles, but also the greater part of the Italian Peninsula. For the direct sovereignty of Milan and Naples carried with it the indirect control of virtually every other state in Italy except Venice and the States of the Church. Nor was this all; for Philip's cousins on the Imperial throne, ruling one-fifth of the Empire in fact and the whole in theory, together with many territories to the east of the Empire, were an integral, and usually obedient, part of his system. To this great aggregation of power must be added the greater part of the New World, together with many miscellaneous possessions on the north coast of Africa and in further Asia. As a Spanish historian proudly remarked, "the Sun never set on the dominions of the King of Spain and at the slightest movement of that nation the whole earth trembled."

Philip, who personally ruled this vast area and population scattered over both hemispheres arrived in the Peninsula in the autumn of 1559 — never to leave it again during the thirty-nine years that remained of his life. During that period his will counted for more than the will of any other man in the world. It is, therefore, of the utmost importance to arrive at a just estimate of his character and policy.

In appearance he was typically German, fair-haired, growing prematurely grey, fresh-complexioned and blue-eyed. He was somewhat below the middle height, but well formed in face and figure. The most noticeable things about his appearance were the placid and rather melancholy dignity of his passive countenance and his Habsburg jaw, which, however, was less noticeable in him than in the majority of his race. His health was habitually poor. He was rarely out of the doctor's hands; though, contrary to many prognostications, he suc-

From Reginald Trevor Davies, *The Golden Century of Spain, 1501–1621* (London, 1937), pp. 117–121 and 126–136. Reprinted by permission at MacMillan and Company, Ltd. and St. Martin's Press, Inc.

ceeded in completing his three-score years and ten before death triumphed.

The character of this man has been the source of age-long controversy. From his own day almost to the present one he had been represented as a monster of iniquity, "the demon of the noonday," a gloomy tyrant, and a religious fanatic ever thirsting for fresh victims to torture and to destroy. This "Black Legend" had its beginning with the famous *Apologia* of William the Silent, which was published for purposes of anti-Spanish propaganda in 1581, and in the *Relaciones* of Philip's traitorous secretary Antonio Pérez, which were published with a like purpose in London in 1594. It rolled on through the centuries, gathering volume like a snowball. For most of the memoir writers, historians and dramatists approached the subject of Philip II with a violent prejudice. Frenchmen, Dutchmen and Englishmen were the inheritors of national hatred. Protestants had even stronger grounds for dislike; and to nineteenth-century liberals Philip was apparently the incarnation of everything they hated — bigotry, autocracy, and the oppression of small nations. The hostile presentation of Philip II had not exhausted itself till the end of the nineteenth century. For two centuries after his death few were found to take up the pen in his favour; and it was not till Ranke in the earlier part of the nineteenth century set an example of investigating foreign archives for the reports of ambassadors and other contemporary material that a different view of Philip II came to light. From that time there ran side by side with the hostile view a strong current in Philip's favour which reached its maximum force in the — perhaps over-favourable — estimates of Fernández Montaña and Charles Bratli. The latter, a professor at Copenhagen, discovered at Florence certain *Relazioni di Spagna*, written by a diplomatic observer contemporary with Philip, which amply confirmed his extremely favourable view.

The final estimate of Philip's character, based on an unprejudiced examination of all the evidence, has yet to be made. Certain features, however, stand out with the greatest clearness. He was an exceptionally dutiful son, a devoted husband, and a singularly understanding and affectionate father. His letters, written to his daughters Isabella and Catherine during his journey in Portugal (1581–3), show a mixture of kindly interest in their childish doings together with a homely humour that is altogether charming. His love for his children is important in view of the accusations brought against him in connection with the death of Don Carlos. Except for a brief period after the death of his first wife, Maria of Portugal, Philip led an austerely moral life at a time when such lives were far from common among princes. Kindness to the poor, an untiring interest in the welfare of his own servants — especially those of the humblest kind — and a zeal for social justice show themselves continually among all the strenuous labours of his long reign. Duplicity and even crime are possibly, though by no means certainly, to be found as incidents in his diplomatic and political life; but such things were no part of his normal behaviour. Those who knew him best recognised him as truthful, devout, frugal in his own living and generous towards others. "There is no one," wrote Giovanni Michaeli, the Venetian Ambassador, "however lowly he may be, who does not find him easily approachable and a patient listener. He is generous; for he grants more than he leads one to hope." Another Venetian Ambassador, Michele Soriano (1559), writes of him: "He has always shown such gentleness and humanity as no prince could surpass; and, although he preserves his royal dignity and gravity in all his doings, as nature and habit incline him, he is none the less gracious for this; on the contrary his dignity and gravity only serve to enhance the courtesy with which he treats everyone."

Philip was a man of comparatively high education and culture and of wide sympathies. He had been taught Latin, French, and Italian by Juan Martínez Silíceo, one of the most famous scholars of his day; and he read and wrote the first of these languages with the precision and facility of a scholar. He was a scholar too in his love of rare and beautiful books, 4000 of which he collected at the Escorial. He derived the keenest enjoyment from music and pictures. He played the guitar with skill and feeling and was remembered as the composer of more than one tune and verse. His care for the collection of pictures and his patronage of artists made the Escorial one of the greatest treasuries of art in the world. In the scanty leisure left him by State affairs, chess-playing with Ruy López — the inventor of the familiar gambit — and the excitement of the chase gave him the relaxation he needed.

By nature he was a pleasure-loving man. "He freely said," Porreño records, "that if he had not been a king he would not have been by choice either a Duke or a Count or a Marquess, but a simple gentleman with a rent-roll of six to eight thousand ducats, so as to be free from the liabilities that fall upon the nobles and great lords." The agency that transmuted Philip's natural character was his conviction of the responsibility attached to the office of king. The doctrine of Divine Right of Kings has been so much reviled and ridiculed by nineteenth-century historians that its good side has often been forgotten. To Philip his Divine Right meant a personal responsibility to God for the welfare of every one of his subjects individually, and, consequently, a passion for social justice and for the protection of the poor against their oppressors. The nobler the office of king the more work and self-abnegation it demanded from the office-holder. Hence Philip set out in life to train himself for the duties of a king. He gradually acquired an iron self-control expressed in immobile features that would register no sign of emotion. He accustomed himself to rise early and work the whole day through so that all the threads of government would be in his hands and his subjects would

escape the injustice and corruptibility of his subordinates.

His father in his many papers of instruction had written one sentence that seemed to be graven into his soul, as though with a chisel of steel into a rock: "Depend on none but yourself."

Every decision, great or small, rested with the king. This was the strength and the weakness of the system. Its strength, in that no favouritism and no undermining of royal power was possible — also bribery and corruption were made difficult, though, as events were to show, not impossible. Philip might have said with Frederick the Great of Prussia: "No one has got *me* in his pocket." The weakness of the system was the inevitable and intolerable delay that resulted from it. For no one man, however early he rose in the morning, could make on time all the decisions required by the governance of a vast empire. Could Philip only have discovered some principle upon which to distinguish the trivial from the important in the business of the day and to pass on the former to subordinates, much might have been well. Philip, however, was developing a new system: he suffered from all the disadvantages of the pioneer; his mistakes were obvious enough to later rulers of Europe who learnt from his example to avoid them. This failure to distinguish between the great and the small was the most glaring fault of his system. The details of some religious procession, the filling of some country benefice, the bridging of some obscure Andalusian stream — such matters as these often occupied hours of incalculable importance, when the very existence of the Empire demanded instant decisions in connexion with such vital matters as the Turkish war, the Revolt of the Netherlands or the Invincible Armada. For everything had to be taken in rotation and sent in a broad circle on its way to a solution. First, the matter for decision would come before Philip himself full described on large broad-margined sheets. Philip would study it and often fill the margins with annotations. He would then send the document on to be discussed by the appropriate council. This in turn would send it back accompanied by many sheets of paper containing their advice. Philip would then study and annotate these and pass on the whole or part to the Council of State. In due course this body would send back the papers accompanied by other papers setting forth their own advice. Philip would then go laboriously through the whole, and after, perhaps, referring back certain details for reconsideration — which meant the further leisurely exchange of paper — Philip would at last make the final decision. The number of papers to be read through and annotated every day which this method of government involved is almost unimaginable. The papers fought an inevitably winning battle against the king. As time went on, the piles of them awaiting attention grew ever larger, and the king, though working almost all the hours of the day and much of the night, was falling ever more and more behind with his decisions, so that the Spanish Government achieved world-wide notoriety for its delays. "If death came from Spain," said Philip's Viceroy of Naples, "we should live to a very great age."

Had Philip recognised the value of speed he might perhaps have found some way to rectify this fatal defect. He did not. He belonged to the type who believe that letters left unanswered for a few months will answer themselves. "Time and I are a match for any two" was an expression of his habitual outlook. Not infrequently he was right. But more often than not, as will appear in the record of his reign, his delays allowed favourable opportunities to slip away, never to return.

The vast mass of papers that have survived, either written or annotated by Philip II, are in their way as impressive a monument as the massive granite pile of the Escorial. His marginal notes are often strangely revealing. They reflect his unhurrying pace and microscopic attention to trivial, and often irrelevant, detail. In one paper written in Latin the writer had spelt the word for "almost" *quassi*. Philip accordingly adds the marginal note, "*quasi* should have but one S." In another the ambassador in London, knowing Philip's avidity for any and every kind of information, describes at length some minute insects that he had seen crawling over his windowpanes. Philip solemnly adds in the margin, "probably fleas." Such entries as these do not, however, convey a fair impression of his intelligence. As a rule his marginal notes reveal a man of sounder sense, clearer insight and firmer grasp of a subject than any of his Councillors.

The events of the last reign had founded the throne of Castille upon a rock. Its overthrow must have seemed impossible. But the most solid rock, as Philip well knew, may be gradually split by the silent and unobserved action of subterranean forces. His policy, consequently, never overlooked the potential danger from the greater nobles. They still ruled like kings over their vast estates. They were still able to raise forces of armed tenants like those which had suppressed the *Comuneros*. Their old ambitious spirit had never been exorcised and their resentment against the growth of royal power was still likely to rise to the surface in a crisis, as Charles V had several times discovered. Philip, consequently, treated his over-mighty subjects with the utmost circumspection. As has been said, he rarely employed grandees in the internal affairs of Spain, and even Alva, the chief exception to this rule, was banished (1578) on the most trivial excuse to his own estates. On the other hand, grandees were freely employed in war, diplomacy, and civil government in distant places, where they would lose touch with their own tenants and with the political affairs of Spain and, probably, cripple themselves with debt. They were also, as in earlier reigns, attracted to the court, where they would be under the royal eye, away from their lands and brought within the influence of royalist sentiment.

The difference between the king and the greatest of these nobles, and between royal and merely noble blood, Philip took every care to emphasise. For this reason, in spite of his love of frugality and simplicity of living, he maintained the elaborate and ceremonious court which he had inherited from his Burgundian ancestors. The enormous number of its functionaries and the stiffness of its etiquette made it both the jest and the model of all the other courts in Europe. The up-rising and the down-sitting of the king were assisted by a multitude of great palace officials, who were the greatest nobles of the land, and who performed in public the most menial offices about the royal person. Grandees, whose ancestors had fought kings on equal terms, now competed for the honour of handing the king his shirt when he rose in the morning, or one of his cups or dishes when he dined in state.

To complete the spectacle of a monarchy high and lifted up above all mere nobles, however long their pedigree or broad their lands, the building of the Escorial was undertaken. There were, of course, many other reasons for the construction on the bleak table-land north-west of Madrid of that giant mass of grey granite which was, in Prescott's famous phrase, at once "palace, a monastery and a tomb." There was, for example, Philip's vow to build a monastery in honour of St. Lawrence, on whose day the battle of St. Quentin had been won (August 10th, 1557), and the fondness, which he shared with many of his family, for living within the shadow of the cloister. There was also the direction in his father's will that his bones should only remain at Yuste till his son had made for them a more fitting sepulchre. Again, there was the fascination which architecture always had for him and his desire for the housing of his art treasures. All these motives had their part in creating that austere and sombre pile among the solitary foot-hills of the Sierra de Guadarrama. But the greatest of all motives was the exaltation of the monarchy above the nobility, which Louis XIV a century later emulated in his palace at Versailles.

The building of the Escorial (1563–84) with its great monastery of Hieronymite monks is a reminder of a very important fact about Philip II, which has often led to a maze of misunderstandings, viz. that he was a devout Catholic. The religious motive moulded his whole character and coloured all his ambitions. He strove to order his conduct and policy according to the teachings of the Church. "It is said at court," reports a Venetian ambassador, "that he enquires of his confessor whether it would be injurious to his conscience to do this or that, and on being told that it would be so, changes the plans which he had been advised to adopt." Like many Spaniards he heard Mass every day, and sought the consolations of religion in the seclusion of a monastery in any great sorrow such as the death of wife or child. Religion upheld him during the long days of ghastly suffering that preceded his death, and made his passing like that of a saint. But it is fatally easy to over-estimate the personal factor in historical causation. Philip's deep religious feeling has, consequently, misled many historians into supposing that his policy was completely dominated by religious considerations; that it turned upon religious bigotry rather than dynasticism, and the extirpation of heresy rather than political advantage. Such a view shows a complete misunderstanding of the man and of the European situation. There were then few persons in Europe, it is true, who would be able to appreciate a clear distinction between religion and politics. To Philip, no doubt, all his policy was consciously directed to the glory of God and the good of his Church; but these things were identical in his mind with the exaltation of the power of Spain. Hence the paradox that Philip in his ordinary policy followed the dictates of political expediency and national interest as unflinchingly as any agnostic — a Napoleon or a Hitler — would have done. Though he was by no means conscious of the fact, his policy was a completely secular one. This is a conclusion of such importance for the understanding of Spanish history that it needs to be emphasised and illustrated.

Whenever political interest and religious zeal clashed, religious zeal almost invariably gave way. It will be remembered that in England he came to the conclusion that the persecution of Protestants was inexpedient. He, consequently, did his utmost to restrain the persecuting zeal of Mary Tudor and to influence opinion against persecution through the preaching of Alfonso de Castro. At the same time his intercession saved Elizabeth's life; and when that shifty princess succeeded to an uneasy throne, Philip exerted himself to the utmost to keep her there in spite of the fact, becoming more obvious every day, that she intended the separation of the English Church from Roman Catholic Christendom. He acted so for the purely political reason that the only alternative to Elizabeth on the English throne was Mary Queen of Scots, an undoubted Roman Catholic but a part of that French system of alliances that was hostile to Spain. For this reason also he greatly strengthened Elizabeth against her Catholic rival by dissuading the Pope from his plans for her excommunication, so that the twelve most critical years were over before the bull (1570) was actually issued — to do more good than harm to Elizabeth's now enormously improved position.

In the same way Philip's relations with the Papacy might well have been those of a completely non-religious statesman. His war against the Caraffa Pope, Paul IV, has already been mentioned. Whatever friendly elements there were in his relations with subsequent Popes was due to subserviency on their part. Few rulers — except, perhaps, Henry VIII of England — have ever maintained so consistently an anti-papal policy over a long period of years. Thus, for example, in spite of repeated protests he stood firmly by the custom that no papal decree might be published in Spain unless it had first been examined by the Council of Castille and that this Council should "hold back" any such decree should it be considered to infringe the laws and customs of the kingdom. In 1572 he went still further and decreed that all papal briefs procured for cases *sub judice* before ecclesiastical courts should be disregarded; and that no Spaniard should be cited to appear before any tribunal outside Spain. Such a decree virtually annihilated the jurisdiction of Rome as far as Spain was concerned. When complaints were made about the interference of Spanish officials in ecclesiastical affairs, the President of the Council of Castille was reported to have said bluntly that there was no Pope in Spain.

The publication of papal decrees was constantly forbidden throughout Philip's reign. Even the publication of the decrees of the Council of Trent was delayed, and when at last (July 19th, 1564) publication was allowed, it was only with the addition of a clause by the Crown that made many of the decrees of no effect. An edict of Pope Pius V (November 1st, 1567) against bull-fights, pronouncing all who took part in them excommunicate, met, as might well be expected, with a far worse reception. Philip consulted a body of Spanish theologians as to the lawfulness of bull-fights. On being assured that these entertainments were not sinful, he disregarded the papal edict — with the loyal support of the Spanish bishops. Such clashes with the Papacy were frequent throughout the reign. When the bull *In coena Domini* was issued (1566) the Pope took the precaution of sending a special brief to the Spanish Bishops ordering them to publish it. The Bishops refused to do so without permission of the Royal Council; and Philip only allowed publication when he was fully satisfied that the bull did not conflict with "the customs of Spain." "You in Spain wish to be Pope and refer everything to the King," was the angry comment of Pope Pius IV. But for the Turkish menace, which made Philip's alliance entirely indispensable, the Popes would probably have shown their resentment in something more than mere remonstrances.

Nor was Philip merely anti-papal in his secular policy. In the domestic affairs of the Spanish Church he was as Erastian as Henry VIII of England. From his predecessors he inherited the patronage of almost all the highest ecclesiastical benefices in Spain and the Indies. He used it carefully so as to ensure the loyalty of the Spanish clergy and to treat them as an integral part of the civil service of the country. His assessor sat in meetings of the National Council of the Spanish Church and his consent was necessary to the validity of any of its decrees. The clergy were constantly requested to assist in any movement the Government had at heart. When, for instance, financial difficulties were unusually stringent the clergy were expected to use their influence in the pulpit and in the confessional to urge the punctual payment of taxes and the abhorrence of all attempts at evasion. The revenues of the Church were scarcely less subject to royal taxation than those of the merchant or the farmer. In short, an anti-clericalist of later times would have differed surprisingly little from Philip in his outward behaviour towards the Church.

In the same way Philip's championship of the Catholic Church abroad might well have been assumed by an agnostic statesman for reasons of pure political expediency. For that Church which in Philip's boyhood had with difficulty maintained herself on the shores of the Mediterranean was in his later life pressing forward — and not without success — towards the mastery of the Baltic. With her doctrines defined and her grossest abuses removed by the Council of Trent, with her faithful Jesuits to form the spearhead of her attack, she had taken the offensive all over Europe. To all appearances the days of Protestantism were strictly numbered. To be the champion of the Catholic Church was, therefore, to fight on the winning side. Furthermore, it was only as champion of the Catholic Church that Philip had any solid reason for interference either in France or in the British Isles. It was the fear of a Protestant succession, with the reversion of the crown to Henry of Navarre, that brought him in his later days within an ace of making France a province of Spain. It was hatred of the Protestant Elizabeth that brought him whatever measure of support he had in Ireland, Scotland, and England. Here again, from a purely secular and cynical point of view, the championship of the Catholic Church was the obviously sound policy.

No less sound from a purely political standpoint was Philip's persecution of heretics. It was taken for granted almost universally in the sixteenth century that more than one religion in one State would bring that State to destruction. There was abundant evidence in support of such an assumption; and persecution in Spain was, in fact, urged as a matter not so much of religious duty as of political expediency. In this the German princes with their principle of *cujus regio ejus religio,* Elizabeth of England with her compulsory *via media* and Philip II were all at one. Moreover, religious toleration can only exist when a large body of public opinion is willing to accept it. No such body of public opinion existed in Spain at the time nor, for that matter, in any other part of Europe. Any ruler in Philip's position, whatever his personal opinions, would have been compelled to choose between persecution and the loss of his throne. It so happened that Philip was able to do with the full consent of his conscience what many other rulers, such as Queen Elizabeth of England, were doing from political expedience alone. But had some cynical agnostic occupied the throne of Spain, obvious expediency would have compelled him to the same course.

Philip's aims were those which almost any ambitious statesman, given his circumstances, would have adopted. He aimed, first of all, at the strengthening of royal power within the various provinces of Spain — a measure of centralisation, sufficient to make all act as one against danger from without, but not enough to destroy that localism which was rooted in the deepest instinct of the country. This postulated, especially, the destruction of all Protestant and Mohammedan movements within Spain, and the reduction of the excessive "liberties" of Aragon. Secondly, he aimed, as so many of his predecessors had done, at the ultimate inheritance of Portugal; and finally, at the domination of the British Isles and France by means of intervention in their religious struggles. In the way of such ambitious plans there were many obstacles. One of these, the Turk, was expected as a matter of course. Another, and far more serious one, the revolt of the Netherlands, took Philip by surprise. Philip's success or failure as a statesman must be mainly judged by the proportion of these aims which he achieved and by the degree of effectiveness with which he attempted to remove these obstacles from his path.

God's Obvious Design and the Winds of God

GARRETT MATTINGLY

Garrett Mattingly (1900–1962) did extensive research in the archives of Western Europe to produce three fundamental books on sixteenth-century Europe — *Catherine of Aragon* (1942), *Renaissance Diplomacy* (1955), and *The Armada* (1959). Sensitively written from the broad vantage point of research in many countries, these volumes have become classics. For the most part Mattingly has been able to transcend national biases and prejudices and has given to his work a rich cosmopolitanism. He has also viewed events and individuals with a sympathetic eye and is, above all, generous and humane in his historical judgments. *The Armada*, from which the selection below has been taken, has enjoyed unusual success both among scholars and in the popular market, a tribute to Mattingly's ability as a stylist. He was until his recent death Professor of European History at Columbia University.

NOBODY since the beginning of history had ever ruled so much of the earth's surface as Philip II of Spain. Nobody had ever owned so many titles of kingdoms, dukedoms, counties, principalities and lordships of all sorts. And nobody, surely, had ever had so many papers to read. Sooner or later Philip read, if not all, at least a very great many of them, leaving in his spidery scrawl in their margins shrewd statesmanlike comments and trivial corrections of spelling and grammar, each annotation a witness to posterity of his appalling, his stupefying industry. Naturally, he sometimes got a little behind. If the message that Mendoza sent off with such haste had remained unread for days and even weeks on the king's desk it would not have been the first dispatch, or the last, to be treated so.

Usually, however, the more important dispatches got fairly prompt attention. Usually, if Philip delayed action, it was because he made a habit of second thought. He liked to review methodically all the arguments for and against a given step, preferably outlined in writing and supported by relevant files. Among his councilors he listened, but rarely spoke. Afterwards, in silence, entrenched behind com-

From Garrett Mattingly, *The Armada* (Boston, 1959), pp. 70–75 and 387–392. Reprinted by permission of the Houghton Mifflin Company and Jonathan Cape, Ltd.

forting stacks of paper, while candles flickered and an under-secretary yawned in a corner, slowly and stubbornly Philip made up his mind alone.

For this trait of the royal character, as for others, the monastery of San Lorenzo de Escorial provides a symbol and a revelation. Philip had dreamed of San Lorenzo while he was still fighting his father's wars in the Netherlands. Even in those first dreams the monastery-palace had always been in Spain. He had begun to search for its site almost as soon as he returned to his kingdom. He had paced the bare hillside above the wretched village of Escorial before a peg had been driven or a trench dug, had drunk from the mountain springs, sniffed the keen air, felt the wind and rain on his cheek. Once decided, he had hurried an army of workmen to the chosen spot, and a somewhat confused and irritated convent of Hieronymite monks along with them. Thereafter Philip could not keep himself away. He preferred this pastoral austerity to stately Toledo or soft, delicious Aranjuez, the parish priest's spare bedroom or an improvised cell in a makeshift wooden monastery to his pleasantest palaces. In the twenty years San Lorenzo was abuilding he constantly pored over the plans with the architect, scrambled about scaffolds with the master builder, and encouraged the workmen with more interest and affability than he ever showed to his grandees. The main outlines of the building and many of its details were intimately his.

Early he had planned for the center of the structure a noble church where his father's bones and his own might lie, and where masses could be said for their souls, many masses daily, until the end of time. From then on Philip seemed obsessed with the fear that he might not live to see his tomb. He pressed the work so urgently that his councilors grumbled about a king who spent as much time on one monastery as he did on all his kingdoms. Now, although the decoration of the interior would never be finished as long as the king's agents could find another painting in Ven-

ice, another tapestry in Flanders or another piece of classical sculpture in Naples or Rome, the last stone had been placed and the last tile laid for more than two years. Philip had begun to live inside his dream. The vast stone pile which he had drawn about him like a garment spoke of his peculiar self as no other building in Europe had ever echoed the spirit of a single man.

The building is seated on the knees of the mountains, the saw-toothed rock ridge of the Guadarramas rising steeply behind it and the rolling piedmont falling swiftly away before. It stands like a monument held out on a pedestal for the admiration of the Spanish plain. In its elevation, its distant prospects, its savage backdrop to the north, and the light and air and silence all around it there is an overpowering sense of solitude, of isolation. The massive, unornamented walls, built of the local granite, might almost have grown up out of the mountain. Their meager, deeply recessed windows might be the mouths of caves or the embrasures of cannon.

At the center of the building rises the dome of the monastery church. Its shape suggests St. Peter's, a resemblance which did not escape contemporaries, which probably was meant not to escape them. Whoever might be emperor by the choice of the German electors, Philip felt that he was emperor by God's election and so a sacred personage, the equal of the pope. The church which says so is smaller than its Roman rival, but there was no stand of buildings in sixteenth century Europe which compared in size with the Escorial except the complex of St. Peter's and the Vatican. Both combined, conspicuously, a palace and a church. Both were, for Europe in the 1580's, modern buildings in the latest architectural fashion. Both breathed the spirit of the Counter Reformation. But here the resemblance ceased. The church of San Lorenzo in Philip's time had none of St. Peter's gaiety and lavish popular magnificence within. It has never had St. Peter's air of open, all-embracing welcome without. Philip's San Lorenzo is shut away at the center of the massive walled monastery like the innermost citadel of a fortress, like a sacred standard in the middle of a phalanx. St. Peter's stands for the spiritual counteroffensive of Rome, the confident, magniloquent advertisement of a catholic faith. The church of San Lorenzo stands for the embattled defense of orthodoxy by the temporal sword.

That the great monastery actually seemed to Philip a defiance and a threat to the heretics of Europe which those wicked revolutionaries would risk anything to spoil is more than a fantasy. He often said so, attributing every accident or delay to the machinations of heretic spies, and a building thought of in those terms could hardly fail to resemble a fortress. That the church at the center should be at the same time a tomb where, according to plans which affected the whole complex structure, masses in overpowering numbers were to be said for the soul of Philip and his relatives, tells us less of the king's spiritual views than it does of his sense of the unique position which he and his family occupied in Christendom — just as the site he selected is eloquent of his elevation above even the greatest of his subjects. But the Escorial reveals more than Philip's public image of his public self. At the secret heart of the great building, right next to the monastery church, a meager suite of rooms is hidden. The most important pieces are a sort of study or workroom decently lighted but somehow meanly proportioned, and off it an alcove bedroom which has a shuttered little window opening into the church near the high altar. Monastery, palace and tomb prove only so many masks concealing a retreat, a refuge, almost a hiding place.

It was not enough that the site Philip had chosen for the Escorial insured isolation. On the bare, rocky slope where he had built it, there was no decent human habitation except San Lorenzo itself, and the use of the land around left no room for any. Moreover, vast as the building was, the king's plans had so filled it with activities, a school, a library, a workshop, a

hospital, that it would barely hold the enlarged congregation of Hieronymite monks and a reduced royal household. There was no room for the swarms of courtiers, of suppliants and projectors who closed in on the king as soon as court moved to Madrid or Valladolid. His overpowering courtesy cousins, the grandees, and the watchful importunate envoys of his clients and allies could neither impose on his hospitality here nor set up their households at his doorstep.

Yet inside the isolated pile Philip had managed a further isolation. The unkingly little huddle of rooms where Philip now spent a longer time each year had been designed to keep people out. The chambers were too small, the corridors too narrow for any crowd. The approaches were easily controlled; the eye could sweep each room at a glance; there was no chance of an unexpected encounter. Philip was an affectionate family man, but his family lodged elsewhere. Philip loved and trusted his monks, but his way into their choir was by a hidden door and a secret stairway. Even the public entrance to his apartments had something closed and secretive about it. Once inside it Philip could enjoy real privacy. In the sixteenth century, as throughout the middle ages, privacy had been the unenvied prerogative of hermits. The greater a man was the larger the crowd in the midst of which he was expected to pass most of his waking life. It was probably his increasing passion for privacy rather than his conventional piety which led people to feel, as he grew older, that there was something monkish about Philip.

In a sense there was. There was true asceticism in the way he toiled, eyes redrimmed, bones aching, fingers stiff, at his self-imposed task of chief clerk of the Spanish empire. Increasingly, as he grew older, he gave up for it not only the hunting, dancing, and feasting which were the conventional diversions of kings, but the things he really loved, flowers and pictures, country excursions, and the company of his children. And there may have been true religious meditation in the agony of doubt with which he confronted every major decision of his reign. We know that he believed God expected more of kings than of other men, and far more of the king of Spain than of any other king. He was conscious of bearing a terrible, a unique burden. Perhaps the solitude of that cell-like cabinet, within sound of the chanting of the Hours, was as necessary to him as he wrestled with the problem of what God wanted him to do as it might have been to the lonely wrestling of any other monk.

THE WINDS OF GOD

Imperturbability in the face of triumph or disaster was a part of the public character of Philip II, a part of his legend in his lifetime. As a small boy he must have heard many times how his father, the emperor, had received the news of the great victory at Pavia with a self-restraint which had aroused universal admiration. Probably he resolved to emulate such behavior, and found it the easier to do so because his temperament was naturally something less than effervescent. At any rate, by the thirty-third year of his reign, Philip had become, for his many admirers, the typical Christian stoic, and a hundred popular stories illustrated his admirable self-control under trying circumstances. Some were like the comic classic about the newly appointed secretary who was so nervous in his unfamiliar duties that when he took a freshly written sheet from the king's hand, instead of sanding it, he poured the inkhorn over it. He cringed in expectation of the royal wrath, only to be told gently, "*That* is the ink. *This* is the sand." Some were like the pathetic anecdotes of the king's long-suffering patience with the growing eccentricity of his first-born son and heir, Don Carlos. There were so many such stories current within a decade of Philip's death that naturally some of his more sympathetic chroniclers found some to illustrate his iron self-control at the moment of his greatest disappointment.

Father Famiano Strada's apologue has the highest literary polish. As he tells it, the king was still nourishing the belief that the Armada was victorious when a courier from Santander (Maestre de campo Bobadilla?) reached the Escorial with the news of disaster. The royal secretaries, Moura and Idiáquez, were aghast, and each tried to persuade the other to break the evil tidings. Finally Moura entered the royal cabinet and when the king laid down his pen and looked up, the secretary stammered something about bad news of the Armada, and thrust the courier forward. The king listened to the dismal tale without a change of countenance and when it was ended, said, "I give thanks to God by whose hand I have been so endowed that I can put to sea another fleet as great as this we have lost whenever I choose. It did not matter if a stream is sometimes choked, as long as the source flows freely." And without a sigh or a change of expression, the king picked up his pen and went on with his letters.

But Strada was, after all, Roman born and bred, and Spanish eloquence at its best is less ornate and has a deeper, more iron-throated clang. Perhaps that is why, from the later seventeenth century on, Spanish historians preferred a variant version. The build-up, the frightened secretaries, the serenely toiling king, the courier's grim news, all these are the same, but before he takes up his pen again, the king says only: "I sent my ships to fight against men and not against the winds and waves of God."

None of these stories, of course, could possibly be true. Philip had no opportunity to display his famous constancy in the face of unexpected disaster because the full extent of the defeat was broken to him by slow degrees. Some time before the duke made Santander, Philip had read Medina Sidonia's letter of August 21st with its accompanying *Diario,* and listened to Captain Baltazar de Zúñiga's depressing report. He had heard both Parma's account of the missed rendezvous and, later, rumors of wrecks on the Irish coast. Nor is it believable that Philip would so instantaneously have blamed the winds and waves of the God his fleet had sailed to serve, especially since he had learned from Medina Sidonia's *Diario* that, up to August 21st, anyway, the Armada had had all the best of it in the way of weather.

That Philip faced the bad news, as it came in, with dignity and constancy one can well believe, though there are limits to the constancy that can be expected of any human frame. He was seriously ill that fall, an illness, in the opinion of the diplomatic corps, brought on, or at least aggravated, by anxiety and disappointment. The new papal nuncio thought that the king's eyes were red from weeping as well as from study, though if Philip wept, no one saw him. And there were those to say that the events of the past ten months had aged the king as many years. It is after 1588 that his skin begins to have that curious mushroom pallor and to hang on his face in pouches. The beard loses the last hint of yellow in its white — is longer, and in some portraits looks curiously neglected. After 1588 the king went outdoors less often, saw fewer and fewer people, worked longer and longer in his solitary study.

But if Philip felt the blow of fate, and showed he felt it, he was not crushed by it. Almost as soon as he learned the extent of his losses he was assuring ambassadors that he would build another fleet stronger than the last, if he had to melt down every piece of plate on his table and every silver candlestick in the Escorial. It did not quite come to that, but American bullion had to be supplemented by scraping the cupboards of Castile and striking new bargains with Genoese bankers. After talking to some of his captains, Philip saw more clearly that it was not just a question of hiring ships. He would have to build his own if he wanted sound ones. And he would have to expand Spanish production of cannon. Recruiting, gun-founding, shipbuilding, financing, the king's industrious pen put them all in train before the new year, and

though things moved slowly, as they do in Spain, and there was much lost time to make up, and many omissions to repair, so that few believed Philip would get his new fleet by spring, nobody doubted he would get it.

Meanwhile Philip had to come to terms with what had happened. The first step was his letter to the Spanish bishops of October 13th. After telling them briefly the news they already knew, and reminding them of the uncertainty of war at sea, he went on, "We are bound to give praise to God for all things which He is pleased to do. Now I give thanks to Him for the mercy He has shown. In the storms through which the Armada sailed, it might have suffered a worse fate, and that its ill-fortune was no greater must be credited to the prayers for its good success, so devoutly and continuously offered." And he tells the bishops gently that the prayers may be discontinued. No more ships were likely to come home. As early as this, then, the defeat of the Armada began to be ascribed in Spain to the winds of God.

It is easy enough to see why the English and Dutch should so ascribe it. "God breathed and they were scattered," runs the legend on one of Queen Elizabeth's Armada medals. A Dutch medal records a similar sentiment, and the learned poets who celebrated in Latin verse the triumphant preservation of the Virgin Queen and the Protestant faith were so busy extolling the divine partisanship which drowned some thousands of Spaniards by a specially provided tempest that they scarcely had time to mention the English fleet.

Of course, better ships and better guns had won the battle before the Spaniards had any trouble with the weather, and even the losses off Ireland were due more to those barrel staves Drake burned at Cape St. Vincent than they were to storms, but the more the destruction of the enemy could be seen as a direct act of God, the clearer it would be that God was a Protestant, and that the common cause was, as it claimed to be, God's cause. So the great storm which destroyed the Spanish Armada joined the other legends, the massacres by the wild Irish, the vast Spanish ships and the tiny English ones, the cowardly Spanish commander skulking in a specially constructed shelter below decks, and the insulted gunner blowing up a galleon and leaping into the sea.

The odd thing is that all these legends are as familiar in Spain as in England, even the one about the duke of Medina Sidonia, "lodged in the bottom of his ship for safety," which the author of *A Copy of a Letter . . . found in the chamber of Richard Leigh* made up out of whole cloth to amuse his fellow countrymen, and the one about the tiny English ships and the vast Spanish ones, which must have begun when some literary landlubber, watching perhaps from the Isle of Wight, compared the swarm of English pinnaces with the ponderous *urcas,* and neglected to notice the fighting ships. At first thought, the hardest to understand is why the Spanish should have adopted the myth about the storm. Naturally, the English welcomed a material proof that God was with them, but why should the Spanish accept the view that God was against them, that their fleet had contended in vain, not against men, but against the winds and waves of God? It is only at first thought that it is hard to understand. It is always easier to accept defeat at the hands of God than at the hands of men, and the Judaeo-Christian tradition is rich in resources for explaining apparently irrational behavior on the part of the Deity. That this time God had let them be defeated did not mean that the Spaniards were not fighting in His cause or that He would not uphold them in the end.

Another seeker for the way of Christian stoicism, Don Bernardino de Mendoza, after he had absorbed the bitter fact of the Armada's defeat, put the point to his master with considerable eloquence and subtlety. Even the noblest crusaders, even

St. Louis, himself, he observed, with pardonable understatement, had not always been victorious. Our sins are so many and so heavy that no punishment God inflicts could be unreasonable, but God punishes those who truly love Him for their good, sometimes in this world as well as in the next. It may be that He chooses to humble those who fight in His cause so that through humility they may learn the way to victory. Philip underlined this sentence and scrawled an emphatic agreement in the margin.

Through humility to learn the way to victory. All that winter Philip's pen probed at the mistakes he had allowed himself to make: the heterogeneous fleet — next time the ships must be better, and up to some uniform standard; the lack of long-range guns — more culverins and demi-culverins, next time; the divided command, the bad co-ordination, the lack of a deep-water port, even the question of how to dominate Dutch coastal waters, the crucial question which somehow Parma had neglected and allowed everyone else to neglect. Philip reached no brilliant solutions, but at least he faced the problem and began to see how much there was still to be done. The shock of defeat had awakened him from the somnambulistic trance into which he had been plunged after the death of Mary Stuart. For the rest of his reign he was again the Prudent King, cautious, even to the point of what looked like timidity, hesitant, watchful, given to second thoughts, providing against every possible contingency as far as he could, before leaving anything to Providence.

There is one more anecdote which sounds authentic and relevant. We have no date for it, but it would be odd if it were not at least a year or two after 1588. Philip was walking in the inner garden of San Lorenzo when he heard the gardener declaring that after so much work done to train the pear trees on the south wall, God simply could not allow the promised fruit to be blighted. Philip called to him in a sterner tone than he commonly used among his monks: "Brother Nicholas! Brother Nicholas, mind what you say! It is impiety, and almost blasphemy, to presume to know the will of God. It comes from the sin of pride. Even kings, brother Nicholas," he went on more gently, "must submit to being used by God's will without knowing what it is. They must never seek to use it."

THREE MODERN DISSENTERS

Tendencies and Individuals: Philip II

SIR CHARLES OMAN

One of the most prolific and vigorous Oxford scholars of the early twentieth century was Sir Charles William Chadwick Oman (1860–1946), whose knowledge of military campaigns and command of historical detail was proverbial. Oman received his formal education at New College, Oxford, and served as a fellow of All Souls College and as Chichele Professor of Modern History. In 1919 he was knighted for his public as well as his academic services. Oman's principal interests were in the fields of military, medieval, and early modern history, where he contributed his well-known volumes on *A History of the Art of War in the Middle Ages* (1898; enlarged and revised 1924); and *The Art of War in the Sixteenth Century* (1937) — both classics. The present selection is drawn from a group of essays which he published in 1937 under the general title *The Sixteenth Century*. Like most of his writing this essay contains the directness, vigor, and bias for which he was famous.

ODDLY enough the great Emperor's detestable son left more of a trace on the history of the century than his brilliant father. The one had been a prince of the Renaissance, the other was a more perfect example of a prince of the Counter Reformation. Considering the opportunities for evil that lay before "el rey prudente," we can only express a feeling of relief that his procrastination and indecision, his distrust of his best friends and his nearest kin, his leaden hand and his faithless pen, his secret treacheries and his open persecutions, saved Europe from falling under the black tyranny of a hypochondriac.

His armies fought many a good fight, his generals were the best in their generation. Fortunately, the inspiration at the centre was missing. Philip himself was neither a general nor an organizer, and the strength which he wielded was due to his father's work, and to the line of great leaders bred in the old Italian wars. He himself, shut up in the Escorial, an ascetic Tiberius in a very bleak Capreae, contributed nothing to his wars but orders difficult and sometimes impossible to execute, always received with dismay by the reluctant commanders of his formidable hosts.

When we say that Philip left a permanent impression on his age we mean that he accomplished the remarkable feat of ruining the great empire which his father had left him, of leaving Spain drained of vitality and condemned to spiritual lethargy. A series of unsuccessful wars, combined with the deadening influence of systematic persecution and espionage worked by the Inquisition, broke the spirit of the Spanish race. Not all the gold of Peru and Mexico would compensate for the loss of initiative and energy caused by Philip's minute and detailed tyranny. For the misfortune of Spain his reign extended over more than forty years — destined to

From Sir Charles Chadwick Oman, *The Sixteenth Century* (New York, 1937), pp. 89–97. Reprinted by permission of the E. P. Dutton & Company, Inc. and Methuen & Co., Ltd.

be almost exactly parallel with those of his shifty and unscrupulous rival Elizabeth of England — he started three years before her (1555 as against 1558); she outlived him by five years (they died in 1598 and 1603 respectively). By the time of his death he had crushed the spirits of a whole generation of his subjects, and left ruin behind him.

Philip, therefore, may be reckoned as one of the dominating figures of his age, though his domination was entirely of the negative sort — he saw to it that the inspiration alike of the Renaissance and the Reformation was killed in southern Europe — having the effective but not always willingly given cooperation of the Counter Reformation popes and the Order of the Jesuits. They would not have accomplished all they did without the help of his sword, nor he have carried out his policy without the aid of their propaganda. But being a single figure with forty years of activity before him, he stands out more prominently as an individual than Paul IV or Pius IV or Pius V, all of whom were short-lived rulers, working for the general end, no doubt, but in ways determined by their personal idiosyncrasies. Between them, Philip, the popes and the Jesuits kept half Europe in the Roman obedience, though the other half slipped free after a final struggle.

It should be noted that Philip was, in the early years of his reign, after the Peace of Cateau Cambresis (1559), in a much more favourable position for exercising general influence in Europe than his father had ever been. The two great hindrances which had stood in the way of Charles V had been removed. France, after the death of Henry II (1560), had plunged into a long series of civil wars, and was "out of the picture." Turkey, after the death of Soliman the Magnificent, had fallen into the hands of incompetent and eccentric sultans. The German problem had been taken out of Philip's hands by the fact that his uncle Ferdinand and his cousin Maximilian successively wore the imperial crown, and had to deal with the situation created by the Augsburg compromise, with which they worked on an opportunist policy, anxious to keep the peace at all costs. They were not of much use to the fanatical Philip, and could not prevent their Protestant vassals from sending intermittent help to his revolted subjects. But on the other hand they took off from his shoulders the weight of the German burden, which had broken down his father's strength. If they gave him little help, they at least guarded his rear, and saved him from any serious interference on a large scale on the part of the German Protestant princes. It may be added that they took over the land-front of Christendom for defence against the Turk, though the Turk was growing very much less formidable than he had been in the days of Charles V.

Absolutely dominant in Italy by virtue of his possession of Milan, Naples, and Sicily, and his predominance over the minor states — the Dukes of Savoy and Parma served as generals of his armies, while the popes had reluctantly dropped their ambitions as secular princes — Philip had no danger to fear in the lands which his ancestors had won by so much hard fighting. Spain was already tamed by his father — the days of the Comuneros and the rebellious feudal nobility were long past. In the middle of his reign Portugal fell into his hands by inheritance — unwillingly, but with hardly a blow struck to preserve its independence, and with Portugal went all its empire in the eastern seas, "the wealth of Ormuz and of Ind," which Pope Alexander VI, with such splendid disregard of other people's rights, had granted to Manuel the Fortunate eighty years back. But the Portuguese colonial empire, great as it was, was far less important than the American empire which the Conquistadors had won for Charles V, while he was engrossed in his Italian wars. The gold and silver of America had begun to pour into the Spanish treasury in the later years of Philip's father, but not in such regularity as was to be the case when exploitation had replaced military conquest. The Emperor had profited from the hoarded wealth of Montezuma or Atahualpa, captured once in bulk and irreplaceable: his son got the regular produce of mines worked systematically by slave labour, a vast annual income. He could depend upon it as a normal item of his revenue, till in the second half of his reign the buccaneering English began to interfere in the Atlantic with the precious ever-welcome flota. The American gold, long the monopoly of Spain, upset all the scale of prices in Europe, when it began to be dispersed around, mainly in war expenses. Already in the time of Charles V it had caused financial troubles in many lands, the gold-owning sovereign having an immense advantage over his political rivals. But Philip was a much greater gold-monopolist than his father: he found ways to get rid of his primary advantage by means of unsuccessful wars and lavish subsidies to allies, till all that was left to him was the fact that prices were higher in Spain than in any other country of Europe, and that national industries flagged, because they could not compete with those of countries where the costs of production were not so abnormally high.

With such resources it might have been supposed that Philip might have controlled all Europe, or at least all southern and western Europe. That he failed to do so was entirely his own fault. He was governed by a curious mixture of obstinacy and procrastination; when he had made up his mind he was hard to move from his resolve, even when circumstances continued to prove that his decision had been unwise. But it took a very long time for him to arrive at any decision, because he profoundly distrusted all advice given him by his ministers or generals. He was always suspecting interested personal motives in any course suggested to him by his subordinates: and their reports, preserved in the Spanish archives, show countless marginal notes arguing criticism and distrust in his own hand. For he read everything, important or unimportant, that came into his chancery, and wasted endless hours in commenting on things trivial as well as on things of real moment.

If Philip had been merely an honest fanatic, ready to wade through any amount of blood, and to kindle any amount of fires for heretics, he would have been much less hateful than was actually the case. But he was also a systematic liar and hypocrite, who thought no means too base to secure his two great ideals — autocratic power for himself, triumph for the Roman Church. He made no scruple of violating the most solemn written engagements — other princes did that in his time — but his habit of subsidizing hired assassins even contemporary opinion thought unworthy of a man of ostentatious piety. He lured suspected persons into his clutches, and put them secretly to death without a trial: suspicion was as fatal as proved treason. But the word treason might be made to cover almost any action that savoured of criticism or disobedience. His chosen tool, the Duke of Alva, once wrote a letter to him which expresses the whole mental attitude of master and man: "Lawyers are only accustomed to pass sentence on a crime being proved: that will never do here." One of his most odious habits was to utilize the Inquisition for his own political interests, where religion was not in the least in question. Indeed, it may perhaps be said that he was a tyrant first, and a fanatic only in the second place. It will be remembered that he dealt most drastically with Paul IV when the old Neapolitan pope ventured to assail him by force of arms and with French aid. But it was seldom that the interest of the autocrat clashed with that of the orthodox Catholic. And his faith was as sincere as his belief in his own essential infallibility — the two inspirations generally worked together with perfect ease when some particularly treacherous scheme was afoot.

A certain additional distaste has — perhaps a little unfairly — attached itself to the unamiable figure of the despot from his unsocial and secretive habit of life — a curious contrast to that of his blatant and boisterous father-in-law Henry VIII of England. Henry loved to show himself off, to advertise his wit, his learning, his taste in costly apparel and in tournaments and pageants, to appear surrounded by a splendid court, and to show ostentatious liberality. Philip disliked all public ceremonials save *autos-da-fe,* at which he was a regular attendant: it was hard to interest him even in the obligatory official shows which attended his third and fourth marriages. He was awkward in company — as had been very much remarked in his father's day, when he was in Germany and Flanders. He had no gracious small-talk such as some kings successfully cultivate, and disguised his unreadiness of speech by a rebarbative affectation of haughty silence. In his mature years he shut himself up for months in the Escorial, where the gloomy bedchamber in which he died looks out on the high altar of the chapel. The habit of mind which induced him to rear this great palace-monastery in a rocky corner of the most uninviting mountain range in central Spain is obvious. He disliked human society, and preferred to seclude himself with a few secretaries in apartments that are more like cells than ordinary rooms. Here he carried out his interminable desk-work in bleak surroundings. Louis XI of France, a spider of the same sort, had at least the lovely countryside of Touraine around him at Pleissis-les-Tours. Philip looked out on nothing but barren rocks — sun-blasted in summer, wrapped in rain-fogs in winter. Here he could in his more hypochondriacal moments practise self-maceration with the celebrated scourge, which he bequeathed on his death-bed to his insignificant son Philip III.

Philip's character explains his failure to be a world power, even in days when France was become a battlefield of civil wars, and Elizabeth of England was practising all her shifty diplomacy to put off her inevitable fight with Spain for as long as possible. If Philip had been wise, he would have declared war on her in her earlier years, while she was still hardly safe upon her throne, and had not accumulated the navy which was to foil the great effort of Spain in 1588. He imagined himself a diplomatist of great finesse — but the English Queen was almost as unscrupulous and quite as cunning as himself. A study of their insincerities is amusing, but leads to the conclusion that her procrastination was politic, and his temperamental and misplaced. He would have been wise to declare war on her in 1568 over the matter of his seized treasure ships, just before the "Rising in the North"; she had given him quite sufficient provocation.

Despite the distractions of his Algerine wars (1559–65) and Morisco rebellion, Philip's main interest was in the furthering of autocracy and the suppression of heresy in the Netherlands. Here both his ambitions were concerned: he was determined to govern the curious amalgam of old Low-Country duchies and counties, not by their ancient customs as his father had done, but by his arbitrary will. And he was also determined to root out the growing Protestantism which had survived the old Emperor's comparatively mild persecutions. He first imposed on the Netherlands as regent his bastard sister Margaret, the wife of Ottavio Farnese Duke of Parma, with Cardinal Granvelle, a stranger from the Franche Comté, as her minister (1560–64). It was wrongly supposed that the change in the spirit of government, and the terrible increase of executions for heresy, were due to Margaret and Granvelle. This was entirely an error: everything done by the regent was under strict orders from Madrid. Protests proved futile, and only led Philip to send to the Netherlands his ruthless general Alva, with 10,000 veteran troops from Italy (1567). Alva practically relieved Margaret of all power, and set to work to govern by the sword, the axe, and the stake. His decisive act, which made revolt inevitable, was the seizure under circumstances of gross treachery of the nobles who had headed the protest to the King against misgovernment in 1565 — the Counts of Egmont and Horn. The former was the victor of the battle of Gravelines, the last defeat of the French in the great war; the latter High Admiral. They were both Catholics of unimpeachable orthodoxy, perfectly loyal to the crown, and idolized by all the nobility of the Netherlands. For the idiotic cruelty of their execution, under a ridiculous charge of treason, Alva was responsible; but he took the precaution of getting the King's leave. Philip signified his complete approval — the counts were kept for several months in prison till the royal mandate arrived (May, 1568). Alva's "Council of Blood" put to death many hundred Netherland nobles and citizens, by no means confining its attention to Protestants: all constitutional protests had become treason. Hence in its earlier stages the Revolt of the Netherlands was not in fact an entirely Protestant movement — some Catholics joined in the rising as directed for the repression of tyranny, not for the protection of heresy. Philip's two foibles cooperated to make the discontent general: many of the old faith disliked tyranny, though they had no love for Lutherans.

It is surprising that Alva's reckless governance by the sword and stake, accompanied by crushing financial exactions, went on for several years before any general explosion. Partial risings backed by German help he succeeded in crushing: the real war only began with the seizure of Brill by the "Sea Beggars" on 1 April 1572, after which it never ceased for the rest of King Philip's life, despite an abortive pacification on terms of compromise made by Don John of Austria, the most moderate of Alva's successors, in 1577. The terms would never have suited Philip; he disavowed the acts of his able and ambitious bastard brother, who was aiming at building up a kingdom of his own in the Low Countries. The war that went on against the unaided Netherlands from 1572 to 1585, and against the Netherlands backed by the parsimonious aid of Queen Elizabeth from 1585 down to the end of the century, was the "running sore" that sapped all Philip's resources, drained his treasury, and finally broke his heart. The only small measure of success that came from all his efforts and intrigues was that the seven southern provinces of the Netherlands were reconquered, and remained in his hands — half ruined by the expulsion of all their Protestant inhabitants. Pressed in between France and the new Dutch republic, they were more of a charge than a profit to Spain. Aware of this, in his last moments, Philip separated them from the Hapsburg monarchy, and bequeathed them at his death to his daughter Isabella. If she had left heirs a kingdom of Belgium would have come into existence two centuries before its time!

Though hampered for the last thirty years of his life with the interminable Dutch War, Philip found energy enough to interfere with the internal affairs of France on the side of the Catholic Leaguers — some of whom promised him the French crown — and to plan a number of attacks on the dominions of Elizabeth of England. His great Armada of 1588 was only the largest and the most unlucky of several naval ventures. At sea he was always unfortunate, and the most humiliating episode of his old age was to see Cadiz, his most important harbour-city, taken and sacked by an English expedition (1596). His pose during his last years was that of the blameless man afflicted by inscrutable decrees of Providence — like Job of old. But he never realized that his own character was the cause of all his misfortunes.

If we designate Philip II as one of the figures dominating the sixteenth century, it is firstly because he might, if his character had been different, have turned the fate of Europe into ways very different from those which his father had tried; but secondly (and this is most important), because he accomplished a definite feat — he left Spain ruined in reputation, finance, and spirit, though when he took over her rule she was by far the most powerful state in Christendom, and had not only Europe but "the Two Worlds" at her feet. I have failed to find in him any redeeming traits save his quite genuine affection for his daughters, and his dislike for the paintings of El Greco.

The Moral Physiognomy of Philip II

LÉON E. HALKIN

Léon E. Halkin, professor at the University of Liège and a member of the Belgian Royal Commission of History, is one of Belgium's most distinguished modern historians. Born in 1906 of an academic family, he attended school at the École Normale Superieur (Paris) and the University of Liège, where he has been a member of the faculty since 1930. Among his numerous publications are: *Le Cardinal de la Marck, prince-évêque de Liège (1505–1538)* (1930); *Charles de Lannoy, vice-roi de Naples* (1934); *Apoligie pour l'humanisme chrétien de la Renaissance* (1941), and *La réforme en Belgique sous Charles V* (1957). The selection printed below was rewritten from an essay he published originally in the *Revue historique* entitled "La physionomie morale de Philip II, d'après ses derniers biographes," CLXXXIX (1938), 355–367.

I NITIALLY, let us first of all look at the king as painters like Antonio Moro have depicted him, as Titian, Greco, and Pantoja de la Cruz have portrayed him. Philip was not a handsome man. He was short in stature, his face was long and narrow, his beard and hair very blond, with large blue eyes, a straight nose, and thick, sensual mouth with the determined protruding jaw (Prognathism) of the Hapsburgs. In the totality of his person a sense of sovereignty is portrayed, a taste for exactness and love of order.

Now let us hear the testimony of the physicians. It is sometimes said that Philip II was a degenerate, a "crowned fool." I think there is in that a prejudice that we must rectify. The king's assumption of the throne was tainted by inbred marriages, mental illness, and various maladies. This burdensome heredity did not prevent Philip from living a full seventy years without abandoning the effective direction of his states to others. In this domain, psychological and at the same time physiological, the king comes out better because he is better known. Even more, we note at times an otherwise benign aspect of psychasthenia peculiar to Philip II. The famous degeneration of the Hapsburgs actually comes after him: he is in a sense the cause of it more so than its victim, while his puny successor, Philip III, born of a fourth marriage of Philip II (with one of his nieces) was truly abnormal.

After having described the physical personality of the king, let us now proceed to the examination of his character. Since Philip wanted to be, in the full sense of the word, Catholic King and Reformer, let us observe him in his religion and in his morals. The ideal of Philip II was to be a religious monarch. "In no really fair manner can one appreciate him if he is not

From Léon E. Halkin, *Initiation à la critique historique* (2nd rev. ed. Paris: 1953), pp. 99–119. Reprinted by permission of the author. [Translated by Mrs. Elly Zoganas Raptou.]

thoroughly familiar with the Catholic idea of the world and of life in general. It would be committing a grave error, indeed to slander Philip, if we attempted so much as to represent him as a hypocrite in matters of religion. It is quite probable that not even the slightest shadow of a doubt, concerning religious truths, ever penetrated this mind totally bereft of daring and even somewhat sluggish." Philip II did not have a philosophic mind. The complete sincerity of his religious convictions can be proved not only by his long life, filled with toils and tribulations, impoverished of pleasures, but also by the heroic patience and complete resignation with which he endured the most dreadful bodily sufferings. Besides, one cannot at the same time be a sectarian and a skeptic.

It is probably on the occasion of the death of his son, Don Diego, that Philip's profound religious feelings are best revealed. The unfortunate father wrote at the time to Cardinal Granvelle: "This is a blow all the more terrible because it follows others close behind. But I praise our Lord for all that it please Him to do: I comply with His Divine Will and I beg that He be content with this sacrifice."

The sincerity of Philip II is none the less evident in his desire to be useful to his subjects, whose fate preoccupies him at all times. Is not the royal majesty in which he is clothed a divine institution for him? What is more, the king is the vicar of God. Defending the throne is, in his mind, defending the altar. The Duke of Alba expresses his master's complete thoughts when he proclaims before a scandalized Catherine de Medici: "The king would rather lose his crown and his life than reign over heretics."

In his monastic retreat at the Escorial, Philip abandons himself to piety (godliness) which together with work succeeds in rescuing him from himself. Like a simple monk, he attends the religious functions. In his room, where he keeps within a hand's reach several mystical and ascetic treatises, a suggestive painting of Jerome Bosch depicts the seven capital sins and their tragic endings. When he has a portrait painted of him, he prefers to hold a rosary in his gouty fingers.

His religious zeal does not judge even the slightest detail as unimportant and leads him to make childish demands. He seems envious of Henry VIII of England, the pope-king, and calls Joseph II the sexton-king. "I think," writes Philip, "that the feast of the Guardian Angel ought to fall on the first of March. Consider whether in the Divine Service of Saint Anne it would not be preferable to introduce the Epistle *Mulierem fortem;* in the Service of the Eleven Thousand Virgins, consider whether we should not include the commemoration of the saint. [. . .] In some of the Missales printed by Platin, we are told in one part that at the services for the dead we should say the *Lavabo inter innocentes* without the *Gloria Patri,* and in other parts that this psalm should not be chanted."

It was even worse when he wanted to assure his passage into the other world: he exacted thirty thousand masses (services) and "as quickly as possible!" For no other reason than for this perpetual service, the ceremonial of which was minutely regulated by the king, a real army of priests was needed. This helps to explain for us that the Escorial, the most remarkable religious foundation of the king, is first of all a monastery protecting a tomb — much more so than a chateau grafted on a throne.

As for Philip's morality, it is impossible for us to ascertain the facts — so "suspect" are the accounts we have which accuse him, so filled with an abundance of details which astound even the most heated imagination. I would not be far from believing the excesses of Philip at certain times in his life — but, unlike his father, Charles the Fifth, who publicly acknowledged his favorites and his illegitimate sons, if Philip had any, at least he never bragged about them.

One would think that his cruelty, at least is not disputable. There again a problem arises. Philip II was neither a heartless monster nor a contented egoist. His critics have gone so far as to hold against him the tragic death of his son Don Carlos, but all that one can actually reproach Philip for in this somber matter was the terrible confinement imposed on an abnormal son by his own father in the name of the state. The fact still remains that the king was usually very tender toward his children. A reading of his private correspondence offers ample proof for this point of view.

Here is, for example, what he wrote to his daughters during one of his rare voyages: "I am so happy to learn that your brother had only a slight fever and that he is already over it. My sister has shown me the drawing of a horse which seems much better to me than his preceding works — tell him so, and you might add that I have some drawing books that I will bring him upon my return. My sister tells me that his portrait is not a very good one, for he looks much better than the artist has depicted him. [. . .] It seemed to me, while examining this likeness of him, that your brother has gotten bigger, but not that he looks better. I would like to see you all in person instead of your pictures. [. . .] I receive good news of you, and I am told that you are getting very big. According to that, you must have gotten a lot bigger, especially you, the youngest. If you have a measure, let me know how much you have grown since I last saw you, and send me your measurements exactly taken on silk ribbons or thread; add to these your brother's measurements. I'll be thrilled to see them, but I'll be even more thrilled to see you all. I hope that God will soon grant me this joy — ask this of Him and pray that He arrange everything so that it may be done soon, and that He keep watch over you as I desire it."

Isn't this charming? This simple and human language is not that of a dry, sterile heart. And if Philip II does not come near the proverbial joviality of a Henry IV, it is that the control he had over his sentiments and the awareness of his responsibilities prevented such an effusion. Like many timid persons, he was eloquent only when he had pen in hand.

Is it difficult to reconcile the violence that characterized the government of Philip II with the kindness that the king showed to his children? Certainly not! Philip believed he was fulfilling his responsibilities in letting the repression of disturbances take on the aspect of a colonial expedition. Scrupulously imbued with the importance of his mission, he used unrestrained severities laid at his disposal by the penal code of the times. There is nothing to make us believe that he nourished the slightest feeling of cruelty. There were in Philip many men — one bred by the teachings of the Gospel, and the other formed by Machiavelli. There was one who read Saint Teresa and sent flowers to his little daughters, but there was also that side of him that burned heretics and punished the "savages," be they Moors or Flemish.

His family letters aside, it must be conceded that Philip II did not at all times radiate joy and cheer. He made of Madrid, which earned him his true greatness, the most solemn capital of Europe, and of the Escorial he made a pious prison, a sort of museum for relics. In spite of Louis Bertrand telling us that, on feast days, the king would ask the seminarians to dance, the life that he led and that his servants had to lead with him was astonishingly plain, simple, and devout, dominated by the frightful calm of a master who no longer remembered having once been young.

Philip lacked those qualities that chiefs of state sometimes achieve through military activity, speech that is eloquent though empty, the talents of the cavalier, or those of the toreador. Charles the Fifth not only knew how, but loved to combat the bull in person; his Spanish subjects esteemed quite highly these deeds that Philip II could not even attempt to equal. The son of Charles the Fifth would take his revenge in the domain of the arts. There was the museum keeper in him. A man so oriented could not help adoring collections. Rich as he was from all the gold from America, he poured his kingly pride into the treasures that he assembled at the Escorial, "the eighth wonder of the world." In the seventeenth century, an elegant poet named Balthazar Gracian was to extol Philip II as the man of taste — a second Maecenas. Here is his eulogistic narrative, translated from the Spanish and commented on by Jean Cassou: "a Portuguese merchant presented to him an earth star, that is to say, a diamond from the Orient, emblem of wealth, astonishing wonder of splendour! And whilst everyone expected Philip to show, if not admiration, at least some note of attention, they heard from him only scorn and disdain. Not that this great monarch would feign inordinate pride and gravity too, but quite simply, one who is fully nurtured in the miracles of nature and of art is not likely to be excited so easily. 'What price for this gentleman's fancy?' 'Sire,' replied the merchant, 'sixty thousand ducats that I exacted for this offspring of the sun are not to be dismissed with scorn.' Philip pressed the man: 'Of what were you thinking,' said he, 'when you gave such a large sum?' 'Sire, I was thinking that there is but one Philip II in the world!' This act, more so than the jewel, enchanted the king, who ordered that the price sought for the diamond be paid, showing the superiority of his taste in this payment and in this recompense."

Such acts are rare indeed in the dull, unvarying life of Philip II. The out-of-the-ordinary never pleased him; the unforeseen quite disheartened him. He disliked voyages because his stay-at-home habits were disrupted by them. He disliked weapons, since he never took part in combat. Nor did he like the long discourses which did not allow for slow absorption and laborious reflection at this secluded study — "the chamber of the king which was the vital knot of the Escorial and of Spain, the center from which Philip wove his cloth and his shroud. From his window he can contemplate the desert while still in bed, and from an ingeniously contrived bay-window,

he can behold the great altar of the basilica."

Thus, in the cell he chose for himself, the king would work days on end, going through all the diplomatic mail, letters, and petitions himself, as if he had only that to keep him busy. It was easier for him to write than to reign. He would scribble, unceasingly, remarks of all nature — political, philosophical, and moral. He would reply in writing to questions that he would raise in his own mind while reading his documents. This activity would satisfy his restless desire to do everything by himself, while at the same time it concealed quite artfully the rickety nature of his mind.

Nothing escaped his scrupulously careful criticism. Family letters, liturgical texts, ambassadors' decisions, all fell under his scrutinizing eye. To his daughter he once wrote, quite seriously, "You tell me, you, my daughter, that your brother has distinguished himself: you probably meant to say your sister, as is shown by what you write further on. You placed an *o* instead of an *a*; you have also omitted a word. You were no doubt in a hurry while writing the letter."

When he undertook the erection of the Escorial, he supervised it in person, through minutely detailed orders, "the transporting of the working crews, the provisions for the workers, the manner of attending to the oxen, as well as the daily diet of the diseased in the hospital: nothing escaped his meticulous mind."

On occasion, he would advise even his ministers to improve their penmanship in their letters. He would carry to extremes his mania of annotating everything he read — so far that in the process of deciphering a certain document, should he come across some name of a place or of a person that was not well written, he would himself take pains to rectify the error. If some passage, however insignificant, seemed obscure to him, he would point this out to his secretaries.

Godefried Kurth, who spent much time at the archives of Simancas, has admirably described how Philip II used to work. "The first document which came to my attention," he writes, "was a Spanish dispatch addressed from Brussels to the king by the Duke of Alba, under date of January 19, 1569. This article, which is number 16 in the file, is partly in code and partly in plain language. In one of the plain passages, the Duke expresses himself thus: 'I have sent Don Fadreque to Anvers in order to post there, in ordinary garrison, a section of recently arrived Spanish troops. They will occupy the chateau. As for the others, he is to confine them in their respective lodgings. In order to punish the irreverence of the inhabitants of Diest and of Leau, I am sending ten infantry ensigns to lodge there, who will live there a certain number of days at the expense of the population. That will serve as an example for the other towns.' This passage has the king's move all cut out for him. He writes in the margin: 'I do not understand this word 'Leo' [sic] and I have never heard of any place by that name. Find out if this is not some word in code, and if it has no other meaning, what might it well be.' And immediately beneath this first note, probably a few days later, he added the following: 'I have since re-examined this passage; it means *y les embio;* all the same, the *s* looks more like an *o* than an *s*.' This, it seems to me, is worth noting. Philip II, upon reading the dispatch, quite suspected that *Leo* must be the name of a town. The context was sufficient indication to this effect. But having never heard of a place by this name, not knowing that such a city existed in the provinces of the Low Countries, the solitary quill-driver is thrown into conjecture and wonders if *Leo* might not be some code word having quite another meaning. 'We shall examine this later with a clear head,' he said to himself, and went on with the other papers. How much time did he need? In his moments of insomnia, did he meditate on this little problem of cryptography that he had just created, or was it only upon returning to his work table and finding there the docu-

ment held in reserve that he must have thought out his attempt at deciphering? I know not . . . The monarch of the states where the sun never sets had not learned that there existed in his duchy of Brabant a city called Leau. And his laborious reflections on the dispatch of his correspondent continuing on their way, he found the answer, poor man! through a philological conjecture, like a professional humanist. Instead of *Leo,* he surmised, it should undoubtedly be read, *les,* that is *to them (a eux).* Thus, the phrase of the Duke of Alba takes on the following meaning: 'In order to punish the insubordination of the people of Diest, I send *them* (to them) ten infantry squadrons.' That is not altogether satisfactory, for in fact the Duke had written *Leo* and not *les* — our royal commentator remarked this himself, since the conjecture allows to remain in the sentence an *y* (meaning *and*) which becomes altogether parasitic. What does it matter! Philip has succeeded in giving a meaning to a sentence which intrigued him. He is content with it, and goes on to other material."

In Philip's cell, on his table, "the machine of the world is brought to a monstrous administrative combination." By rationalizing over the news, and overburdening the dispatches to his ministers with his own commentaries, the king would hold off the moment of decision. He could make up his mind on events only without directing their course. Thus, history is not made "to order" — only historians reconstruct the past in this way — and one might well have expected Philip to be anything but a king of archivists, a crowned bureaucrat. It seems he was dazzled by the secrets of his government, and his real error was that "in being able to see everything, he was able to prevent nothing."

His ambition, of which he had a great deal, was ill-supported by his irresolute temperament. The too meticulous care that he brought to the preparation of all his undertakings prevented him from acting quickly. He was not able to intervene in good time to protect Mary Stuart; he launched the Invincible Armada against Elizabeth too late; and in France he did not uphold the League until after it had been dishonored by his own excesses.

"Time and I," Philip would say, "we are worth two more." He was mistaken. By dint of wanting to enclose all public affairs in his solitary and concentrated mind, to turn them over within him and to wait unceasingly for the propitious moment, he would usually let this moment pass by without putting it to good use, and even in the most important circumstances. It is in this manner that he possibly could have saved Don Carlos, if instead of silently observing him over a period of several years he had been able to take it upon himself to act with promptitude and energy. It is in this way that he could have conjured up the ruin of the Low Countries, if instead of taking recourse to rigorous measures with the Duke of Alba too quickly and taking recourse to means of reconciliation with Don Juan too late, he had decided to go there in person from the beginning. Granvelle himself could not keep from making this harsh remark about his master: "In all his affairs, his sole decision consisted in remaining eternally indecisive."

Philip II was not a man of action comparable to William of Orange, his enemy, or Don Juan, his brother, or even to his best military leader, the famous Duke of Alba.

He was so jealous of his authority that those who praised the youthful Alexander Farnése caused him much lost sleep. The letter of revocation of this excellent general had been revised three times. Fortunately, Farnése died before knowing the extent of his disgrace.

This act reveals the darkest aspects of the king's character: envy, dissimulation, harshness. Thus, I think that all these faults which are inseparable from Philip's sense of duty and his Christian ideal cannot be sufficiently explained by pride, or incompetence, or by any other external circumstance. Only one, insignificant (though formidable in a monarch) qualm

of conscience, can in my opinion give us sufficient reason: and that is, scruple (or conscientious doubt). Yes, it is the scruple of Philip II — the scruple that Louis Bertrand mistakes complacently for a virtue — which led him to absurd labor, unworthy of a king. It is the vice of scruple — anxious and unreasonable uncertainty, which made Philip restless, uneasy, and worried (in spite of his apparent calmness), slow by horror of precipitation, cruel by fear of weakness, suspicious and inflexible so as not to be duped, in one word, miserable!

"Much more than my wounds," Philip II groaned while dying, in horrible pain, "my sins make me suffer." At the time of the Last Rites, while confessing, he addressed the priest in these words: "Father, you hold the place of God. It is therefore in His Divine Presence that I declare myself ready to do all that you deem necessary for the salvation of my soul. I will place all my good will in this effort, and, consequently, if I should omit something, you would be the one responsible for it." These last words are significant: they throw light upon the infirmity that Philip's religion and his character suffered. He needed, for the fate of his soul, as for that of his state, guarantees in good and faithful form!

Philip II was afflicted by "mental ruminations." How many psychasthenics are there — let us say "scrupulous persons" — whose lack of power over their superior faculties is betrayed by a crise d'efforts, a sudden mania for research, backward retreats, repetitions, conjurations, and other things! All these symptoms, we find in Philip, whether in the case where he imagines he does not understand even the most lucid discourse without rereading the text several times, or in satisfying his mind by incoherent and pacifying conjectures, or finally, in admonishing his confessor to carry the weight of his soul.

Philip II — who seems to have been fully aware of his condition — could have been cured of his scruple as even the least of his subjects. But he was king. He would have needed, at the very least, a confessor with much good sense and some good will. But, he had three of them, for his perdition! And I shall say nothing of the physicians and psychiatrists of the time . . .

Thus, this great scruple of his can alone give us the key to the character of Philip. It is neither that of a monster, nor a saint, but a man of duty, morose, fearful, timid, and sincere, torn between a thousand difficulties and ill-served by a mediocre intellect. The king's taste for petty things and small intrigues was no substitute for either the *esprit de finesse* that is indispensible to great works, or the self-control that gives purpose to a man's life. One ought to be able to render justice unto Philip. But one cannot succeed in liking him.

He lacked a commanding spirit. Indecisive athlete that he was, he did not possess rapid reflexes. Circumstances, nevertheless, made of him an autocrat, both his own misfortune and that of subjects. In a country where a constitution did not exist, he incarnated royal dictatorship in all its horror. At a time when there was no liberty of conscience, he personified state absolutism with all its cruelty. Of this overwhelming role, he is the primary victim, worthy of our pity more than our hatred, the captive slave of absolutism and theocracy.

And yet, the reign of this wretched king was grand and glorious. Grand it was, because of this crusading fever that only Philip, of all the princes of the Renaissance, desired and was able to give to his rule. Glorious, certainly, thanks to the real qualities of labor, courage, and fidelity to his ideal; thanks also to the wars of religion and to the dynastic quarrels which were weakening France, and at the same time England; thanks especially to the influence of Charles the Fifth, who, from his retreat

of Yuste, had ordered the first steps of his successor. Philip II had benefited from the politics of his father. He inherited much of his program and even his advisors. The great successes of the Spanish reign are the work of Charles or his confidants — in the diplomatic field, the marriage of Philip to the queen of England, Mary Tudor; in the military realm, the victories of Saint-Quentin and of Lepanto, one won by Emmanuel-Philbert of Savoy, one of the emperor's generals, and the other, by his illegitimate son, Don Juan.

Philip II forsook his father's policies because of the narrow nature of his character. Rejecting the pointed lessons of the emperor, Philip neglected the study of foreign languages which might have, perhaps, permitted him to understand his subjects from the countries "down there." More pious than Charles the Fifth, he attached himself with more force, but often maladroitly, to the defense of the Catholic faith. Many historians have credited the church with Philip's zeal, while others have bitterly reproached that institution for having nourished his fanaticism. Let us not judge by the Christian ideal . . . his painful caricature. Philip II was prudent, devout, and penitent, but where are his simplicity, charity, and joy?

This Catholic king sincerely wanted to imitate the king of France, Louis IX. By his dissimulation, his harshness, his inquietude, his narrow-minded devotion, does he not evoke Louis XI, of sinister memory, much more so than Louis IX, the humble and pacifist monarch? And it is, undoubtedly, because he was much too scrupulous that, through one final contradiction, Philip II evokes not so much the saintly Louis, as Louis XI without scruples.

The Personal Character of Philip II

CECIL JOHN CADOUX

A noted English theologian and pacifist, Cecil John Cadoux (1883–1947) was a firm believer in moral absolutes. In the works of R. Trevor Davies, *The Golden Century of Spain* (1501–1621) (London, 1937) and William Thomas Walsh, *Philip II* (London, 1938), he saw a dangerous tendency toward moral relativism. This ultimately led him away from his favorite topics of pacifism and theology to a study of the problem of moral judgments in history, the subject of his last book. In this work, *Philip of Spain and the Netherlands*, he took a strong stand, both against the Prudent King and moral relativism. He was, however, more sophisticated in his approach than either Watson in the eighteenth century or Motley in the nineteenth. Cadoux argued that sin or evil must be exposed but that the act can be divorced from the individual perpetrating the act. In other words he found it possible to condemn immorality at the same time he explained it historically and excused the evildoer. To Cadoux there was no problem whether to judge motives or effects; he judged effects. At the time of his death in 1947, he was Professor of Church History and Vice-Principal of Mansfield College, Oxford.

I T MAY possibly occur to some of my readers that, in insisting at the end of the last chapter that the Duke of Alva was a cruel and bloody man, I have been guilty of forgetting the self-denying ordinance which I imposed on myself at the beginning of this book, namely, that I would confine myself to a characterization of evil deeds only and not venture to cast blame on the doers of them. It is a fair question whether to call a man cruel and bloody does not amount to a personal condemnation of him. It certainly does approach very near to that. Yet on the whole I am disposed to defend myself against the charge of breaking my own rule. I can recall a prominent Biblical character who is said to have "shed blood abundantly," but is yet called "a man after God's own heart"! As for cruelty, I am at a loss to know how we can refuse to describe Alva's actions as cruel — and equally at a loss to see how cruel actions can be done by one who is not himself cruel. But I have not presumed to pass any sort of final judgment on the man himself. His personal piety is, of course, unquestioned; and his own reading of the duty that lay before him must be assumed to have been conscientious. If he needs to be condemned in the sight of God, it is for God to pronounce the verdict. To describe him as cruel and bloody in his actual deeds is not necessarily to usurp that function.

The same distinction must be kept in mind as we discuss the character of Alva's royal master. I shall try to limit myself to describing those features of Philip's character which can be observed in, or inferred from, his known actions, without undertaking to administer moral blame. I should endeavour to observe this self-restraint even if the *whole* of these knowable features were repellent: loyalty to it is still more incumbent upon me seeing that there is admittedly much in the picture which is not repellent. The general view of Philip traditionally taken by Protestants — a view founded on the horror which so much of his activity naturally rouses in Protestant

From Cecil John Cadoux, *Philip of Spain and the Netherlands, An Essay on Moral Judgments in History* (London, 1947) pp. 111–133. Reprinted by permission of the Lutterworth Press.

bosoms — is one of unrelieved condemnation. It is only fair that we should be willing to take note of other aspects of his life, those not directly connected with the suppression of Protestantism, which — looked at in isolation, and judged on their own merits — permit a much more favourable judgment to be passed.

It must for instance be patent to anyone at all closely acquainted with the details of Philip's reign that he was a deeply religious man, sincere and assiduous in his worship and possessed of a strong trust in the Providence of God and a very high sense of personal duty. It is true that his religious devotion involved a profound veneration for relics of the saints: but this was an aberration inseparable from a strong adherence to the Catholic view of things, and one from which Philip's education could hardly be expected to have freed him. He exercised an extraordinary self-control over his feelings: very rarely was he seen in a rage; and the patience he displayed under his disappointment at the failure of the Armada and under the terrible sufferings of his last illness was truly amazing. He had a love of social justice as he understood it; and he endeavoured to secure it for his subjects. The confession made on his deathbed that he was not conscious of having ever wilfully wronged anyone, could not but have been uttered in complete seriousness; and it serves therefore at least to illustrate what his own intentions and aspirations had been.

As a family-man he was affectionate. He has been accused of having caused his eldest son Don Carlos to be put to death: but there is no conclusive evidence that he did so. The exceptional measures he took with regard to him (depriving him of his freedom, and so on) can be readily explained by the peculiar difficulty with which the morose and degenerate character of the prince faced him. When no reasons of state called for severity, he was kindhearted and charitable to those in need. He behaved with generosity in the Flemish famine of 1556, and on occasions of public calamity in Spain. When St. Quentin was sacked in 1557, he ordered that the women and children should be spared. He washed and kissed the feet of the poor. He regretted the sufferings needlessly inflicted on the unfortunate Moriscos and on the inhabitants of captured Maestricht.

The habitual solemnity and taciturnity of his demeanour was naturally accentuated at times of defeat or bereavement. Hence has arisen the customary Protestant idea of him as a morose and gloomy recluse. This is no doubt an exaggeration; for Philip, though his manner was not characteristically genial, was a patron of art, literature, and music; he played the guitar, loved flowers and scenery, and was fond of dancing and hunting. Dr. Walsh is at great pains to correct the Protestant impression by adducing evidence along these lines; and we may accept his verdict — though the instances he quotes shed a rather strange light on the ethical judgments both of hero and of biographer. In proving, for instance, what a good hearty fellow the king really was, he describes how he once asked for a boar to be let loose in an enclosure, how he went hunting it in a coach, how monks watched the fine sport from the windows, and how "the boar gave a good account of himself, and disembowelled a horse with one of his tusks before he was slain." He could, moreover, write simply and sweetly to children. During his stay in Portugal in 1581–83, he wrote delightful letters to his two young daughters, Elizabeth and Catherine, in Castille, telling them on one occasion about a nice auto-de-fé that he had witnessed at Lisbon, and how he had been in the same house as the secular judge who was going to sentence those condemned by the Inquisitors to be burnt. He had come away as soon as the sentences were read, and had not been over-tired by the labour of watching and listening.

Conscientious and diligent in discharging the affairs of state, he was painfully slow and inefficient in his methods. Nearly all negotiations between himself and his ministers were carried on in writing. Instead of delegating large authority and responsibility to competent administrators, he kept far too much of the departmental duties of government under his own personal control. The absolute character of his rule discouraged the spirit of inventiveness and initiative in his subordinates. Furthermore, he was at times unwise and unfortunate in the choice of his agents — a fact illustrated by his insisting on the appointment of the inexperienced Duke of Medina Sidonia to the command of the Armada. Closely allied to the temperamental defects just mentioned was the cynical distrust and jealousy which he felt and displayed towards the more gifted of his servants, and his lack of a sense of gratitude towards those who had rendered him signal service. Without presuming to decide whether or not Don John's death was due to Philip's contrivance, as has been believed by many, we observe that even Dr. Walsh realized that Philip was jealous of the loyal Duke of Parma, who, though never given a free hand, had virtually saved the southern half of the Netherlands for him.

It must in fairness be reckoned to Philip's credit that, unlike his father (who, however, warned him against the evils of war), he was an habitual lover of peace. He constantly endeavoured to gain his ends by persuasion and bribery rather than by appealing to arms. It may, of course, be plausibly suggested that he shrank from waging war, not so much from feelings of humanity, as from a cautious and parsimonious dislike of the expensiveness and risks of armed strife. And it is clear that, when roused, he did not shrink from bloodshed. Yet some measure of credit may fittingly be allowed to him for preferring normally to exhaust the gentler means of political pressure before resorting to arms.

Something perhaps should now be said about Philip's relations with women. In November, 1543, when he was not yet seventeen, he was married to his cousin Maria Manuela of Portugal, who in July, 1545, bore him the misshapen pervert Don

Carlos, and died a few days later. Between this time and his marriage with Mary Tudor in 1554, Philip lived for several years in adultery with his mistress Doña Isabel de Osorio, by whom he had several children. In July, 1554, he married Mary of England, who was then thirty-eight years old — eleven years his senior. Whatever may have been the bride's feelings towards her husband, on Philip's side the union was certainly no lovematch. He entered into it, in compliance with a scheme devised by his father the Emperor, for the purpose of strengthening the Hapsburg-monarchy and the Roman Church: and although, with Stoic self-control, he did, while in England, all that could be expected of a newly-married husband, his heart was not in it. During his prolonged sojournings in the Netherlands later in Mary's reign, stories were afloat of his gallantries with the young women of the country; and there was enough verisimilitude about them to arouse the poor queen's jealousy. Allowance must, of course, always be made for the unreliability of gossiping rumour, "upon whose tongues continual slanders ride"; and on this ground some of Philip's apologists are disposed to acquit him of all or virtually all extra-marital immorality. On the other hand, gossip is not always untruthful. Moreover, Philip was a handsome young Spaniard, living in an age when royal irregularities with women were common and were easily condoned; and he is well known to have been extremely fond of dancing and of female society. It must therefore be regarded as more probable than not that his life in the Netherlands between 1555 and 1559 was marked by some licentiousness of conduct. Mary died in November, 1558. In 1560, shortly after his final return to Spain, he married Princess Elizabeth (or Isabel) of France, who was then fourteen or fifteen years old. He was very fond of her, and she gave him two daughters (the children to whom he wrote from Portugal). To his great sorrow she died in October, 1568. The rumour embodied in William of Orange's "Apology" of 1580 to the effect that Philip had had her poisoned is unconfirmed and improbable. It was, however, very shortly after this bereavement that, for the sake of having a male heir (the impossible Don Carlos having recently died), he agreed to marry his niece Anne of Austria: the marriage took place in November, 1570. Anne bore several children, including the prince who succeeded his father as Philip III. She died in October, 1580. "The widower," writes Dr. A. W. Ward, "with characteristic promptitude offered his hand to her younger sister Elizabeth . . ." — a fact which, I think, Dr. Walsh does not mention. No further marriage, however, took place. Late in 1590 rumours were afloat at the French court to the effect that Philip's ambassador at Rome had begged Sixtus V (who had died in August that year) to allow Philip to marry his own daughter Isabel Clara Eugenia — a union which would have fitted in well with his claim to the crown of France (Isabel's mother having been Elizabeth of Valois). Torn between the inherent improbability of so incestuous a plan, and the implications of belief in it on the part of at least two French ambassadors, we may perhaps give Philip the benefit of the doubt, and not press the appalling charge against him.

The character of Philip, therefore, as so far considered, while not wholly admirable, was not without its estimable features. When, however, we attempt to isolate for special study those practices of his which arose directly from his aims and purposes as a Hapsburg and a Catholic, the picture is far less pleasing. Considerable allowance must of course be made for the immense bias imparted to his mind by heredity and education. Over and above that, there comes the peculiar character of political responsibility, which never makes it easy for the holder of it to act on precisely the same principles as those which bind him in his private capacity. Political ethics constitute a thorny and difficult problem; and most rulers, however conscientious and charitable they may be, find themselves faced with ethical dilemmas of a kind that does not usually trouble the ordinary man. Many of these dilemmas, though by no means all, are connected with the coercive activity incidental to all political administration. That is why the records of nearly all rulers, including many possessed of great personal virtue, are marred by acts of severity and deceit and by other moral blemishes.

To this general truth Philip II was no exception. On the contrary, his very conscientiousness lent such strength to his political and religious convictions that they led him into violations of the moral law even greater than a less thorough doctrinaire would have ventured to commit. His ambition was in a word both conscientious and boundless. He was ambitious to preserve and increase his rights as an absolute sovereign. He was ambitious to promote the interests of Spain, to cover the house of Hapsburg with glory, and — by annexing neighbouring states to his crown and family — to enlarge the area of his dominions. He was ambitious to strengthen the hold of the Roman Church on the minds of men, and to destroy whatever might tend to undermine it. These ambitions were so sacred to him that, in pursuance of them, he was prepared not only to do things from which a private person ought certainly to refrain, but to go to extremes which less serious rulers would never have had the hardihood to reach.

Of these more glaring transgressions, we may mention first Philip's various illegal acts. Allusion has already been made to the repeated violation of his twice-taken oath to observe the ancient charters guaranteeing local liberties and privileges in sundry cities and districts of the Netherlands. But breaches of the constitutional law were continually occurring in Spain also, and were a constant topic of protest on the part, for instance, of the Cortes of Castille.

It is, however, in his capacity as a persecutor that he exhibits his ruthlessness most conspicuously. We have discussed at an earlier point in this study the question as to whether his motives in persecuting were religious or political; and I have hazarded the opinion that they were at least in large part religious. Yet it is also certainly true that they were in part political. The idea then current was that kings were appointed and established by God: and it was easy, therefore, for Philip to get the idea fixed in his mind that it was God's Will, not only that he should be king of Spain and master of its dependencies, but that his monarchy should be as strong and glorious as he, with God's help, could make it. But to attempt to disentangle the religious and political elements in his passion as a persecutor is for that very reason a hopeless and artificial task. Not only was he the king of Spain; he was also a firmly convinced Catholic: and the two ideals coalesced into a dominating unity. Spain was to support the Catholic Church, and the Catholic Church was to support Spain: both causes were dear to the Almighty's heart. As we study Philip's persecuting measures, we see now and then the political motive dominant, perhaps more frequently the religious: but they are conjoined in the closest possible manner; and it is only occasionally that anything like a tension between the two is discernible. He felt conscientiously certain that God had charged him with a sacred mission — to glorify the House of Hapsburg, and to destroy Protestantism.

With such ideals fixed in his mind, he drew the conclusion that no considerations of mercy (which, had nothing else been at stake, would doubtless have weighed with him) could be allowed to stand in the way of the zealous fulfilment of his divinely-given mission. Nay, nothing less than the full range of the coercive power of despotic rule was to be employed in its service. It is this thoroughgoing policy which makes the story of his reign such terrible reading; and all the efforts of his apologists to emphasize his more amiable qualities, and to depreciate the character of his enemies, do not avail to render his severities other than

most repulsive. However kind-hearted he might be in his immediate personal relationships, yet where the interests of his monarchy or the interests of the Roman Church were involved, he was utterly merciless. Within the frontiers of Spain he revived and vigorously maintained the Inquisition — an institution whose hideous cruelties and calamitous results have been described in an earlier chapter. He several times attended the auto-de-fé: whether he personally witnessed the burnings (as some Protestant writers have perhaps rashly assumed) or always withdrew before the sentences were carried out (as Dr. Walsh is at great pains to represent as probable), makes little difference. The burning was done in the presence of large crowds, and with the king's knowledge and full approval. At an auto held at Valladolid in October 1559, one of the victims — as he was being led away to be burnt alive — shouted out a protest to the king. Philip replied, "If my son were as wicked as you are, I would fetch the wood to burn him myself." The story of how he drenched the Netherlands with blood has already been summarized. In other countries he fomented civil strife, not shrinking from the misery and desolation he was thus promoting. To the enormous volume of human suffering thus occasioned, he seems to have been totally indifferent. Not only did he urge Catherine de Medici to chop off the heads of the leading Huguenots in her kingdom; but when, twelve years later, many thousands of Huguenots were brutally slain in the massacre of St. Bartholomew, Philip rejoiced on hearing the news.

Other sovereigns have felt themselves under the necessity of coercing and punishing troublesome subjects. But without forgetting this, or departing from our recognition of the religious basis of Philip's policy, I do not see how, with the facts before us, we can do other than describe him as a cruel and intolerant bigot. He was totally unable to understand or respect any convictions that differed from his own. If that does not constitute a man a bigot, what does the word "bigot" mean? How far, if at all, he was to blame for being so, I do not undertake to say: but the fact cannot, I submit, be truthfully denied. Similarly, if his ruinous proceedings do not deserve to be characterized as cruel, I know not where in history cruelty is to be seen.

Murder, says the Christian conscience, is always a crime: but, it normally adds, not all killing is murder. The mutual slaughter of armed men in war, for instance, even when condemned by pacifists on moral grounds, is not for the most part seriously equated even by them with murder. As for the non-pacifist majority, the normal member of it would agree with Iago in confessing:

Though in the trade of war I have slain men,
Yet do I hold it very stuff o' the conscience
To do no contrived murder: . . .

The judicial execution of the legally sentenced criminal is another widely recognised instance of "killing no murder." In ancient Greece, to kill a "tyrant" (i.e., a man who by force established himself in supreme political control of a community, in defiance of the laws), whether it would have been normally designated φόνος or not, so far from being censured or criticized as a moral offence, was lauded to the skies as a conspicuous act of virtue and heroism. Whether tyrannicide was morally right or wrong was one of the great questions which exercised the minds of Churchmen and others during the Middle Ages. The death of the usurping Duke of Orleans in 1407 by contrivance of the Duke of Burgundy effectually stimulated the discussion. Opinion remained divided: but the fierce antipathies roused by the ecclesiastical strife of the sixteenth century both multiplied instances of assassination, and called forth at the same time — especially on the Catholic side — a willingness to defend the morals of the practice. A Spanish Jesuit, Juan de Mariana, wrote an elaborate treatise, entitled *De Rege et Regis Institutione,* which he published in 1599 and dedicated to Philip III, and in which he justified

tyrannicide. To pass from regarding a monarch as a heretic to regarding him as a tyrant was an extremely easy step: and if heresy justified killing a king, how much more would it justify killing a person of inferior rank.

Here then was one chain of reasoning which might well convince a man of Philip's mentality that, if he could compass the assassination of persons like William of Orange, Elizabeth of England, and Henry IV of France, he would be offering service unto God. But there was another consideration which chimed in with this general acknowledgment of the justifiability of killing heretics — and that was the absolute monarch's presumed autocratic right of inflicting the death-penalty upon a guilty subject. As the fountain of justice, the king was regarded as fully entitled to order, on his own authority, a private execution as the judicial penalty of a legal offence.

Mr. Trevor Davies says: "Philip, no doubt, shared with nearly all his contemporaries a belief that assassination for reasons of State was justifiable." Now in a period of desperate conflict, a scheme of assassination is liable to suggest itself at almost any time to one or other of the parties involved: and instances of such schemes may be cited from almost any epoch of history. During the sixteenth century, when — in the cause of ecclesiastical loyalty — the most passionate feelings were aroused, the instances are rather more frequent than at other times. But even so, I should regard it as an overstatement to say that at that time the "belief that assassination for reasons of state was justifiable" was accepted by nearly all Philip's contemporaries. It was, even in that sanguinary age, a desperate expedient, to which recourse was had only in most exceptional circumstances, and which was usually shielded with care from the public eye, not only for the purpose of ensuring success, but also because it was realized that a certain moral stigma was widely felt to cling to it.

Philip's own record in the matter is hard to grasp with any fullness and precision, chiefly because of the secrecy in which he would naturally wish to shroud all such proceedings. A certain number of schemes of assassination are laid to his charge, of which it is impossible to prove him guilty, and some of which are definitely improbable. Examples are the deaths of his wife Elizabeth of Valois and of his son Don Carlos. A court of law would have no option but to acquit him on these charges. But the historian's responsibility is not quite that of a court of law. While the historian must not categorically affirm that a man has committed an evil act unless there is fairly convincing evidence that he did commit it, it cannot reasonably be demanded of him that, before he records his judgment, the evidence should be of the same degree of cogency as a juryman in a murder-trial would rightly insist upon. On the other hand, it is not open to him, as it is to the juryman, to say "Not guilty" whenever the data, though suspicious, fall short of legal proof. In such cases, his duty — unlike the juryman's — may well be to say "Probably guilty." Some of the instances charged against Philip are of this nature. Philip's general character, attitude, and policy are, for the historian, part of the evidence bearing on each particular case. Thus, granting for the sake of argument, that he did not, in point of fact, contrive the deaths of Elizabeth his wife and Carlos his son, we may well ask the question, Is nothing whatever as to his views on assassination to be inferred from the fact that his contemporary William of Orange thought it wise, in a document laid before the eyes of the world, to charge him with murdering them? William's alleged spite or savagery in making the charges is on this precise issue not to the point. The fact that even false charges were made under such circumstances, while it does not make them true, is — in view of other things known about Philip — not without its significance for history. We may safely say that there is nothing inherently unlikely in Philip having secretly had *any* person put out of the way, whose life he regarded as prejudicial to the security and well-being of his throne, his person, or his Church.

I have already described at an earlier point in this study the secret destruction in a Spanish prison in 1570 of the life of the Baron of Montigny, whose death was then publicly declared to have been due to fever. Nominally it was a judicial execution, for Alva had already condemned the man to death in his absence. But the secrecy of the proceeding, and the lying report published about it, indicate surely that Philip shrank from the judgment which public opinion would pass on it.

On March 31, 1578, Escovedo, secretary and envoy of Don John, was stabbed to death in a street in Madrid, by contrivance of his friend Antonio Pérez, the King's confidential agent. In later life, Pérez asserted that he had acted on the king's orders, but that Philip nevertheless persecuted Pérez, because both of them were in love with the widowed Princess of Eboli. A large literature has grown up around the question as to Philip's guilt or innocence regarding Escovedo's death. There are indeed strong grounds for suspecting his privity: but it would be foreign to our purpose to undertake a discussion of the mysterious problem. Nor can we investigate the question whether Philip did or did not cause the premature death of his illegitimate half-brother Don John in October, 1578. The incidents are covered by our remarks on the previous page. Pérez's escapades, however, led to a clash between the Aragonese and the Inquisition. The rebellion was crushed; and Philip ordered the Justicia of Saragossa to be executed in defiance of the law entitling him to be tried by the Cortes of Aragon. Later he made several efforts to get Perez himself assassinated.

In the case of William of Orange, Philip made repeated efforts to get him put to death by the hands of an assassin: and, in view of the part William took in organizing resistance to the king, and in view of the way Philip would inevitably feel about it, one can hardly be surprised. Allusion has already been made to Requesens' part in these schemes. In 1577, when Don John was in the Netherlands, the king approved of a suggestion sent by Pérez to Escovedo that the latter should think out some means of getting the Prince of Orange put to death. In 1580, at the suggestion of Cardinal Granvelle, Philip signed and caused to be published in the Netherlands a royal proclamation denouncing William as a traitor, miscreant, and enemy of his country, encouraging anyone who could to injure him in property or life, and offering 25,000 crowns, noble rank, and a free pardon of any crime, to anyone who would deliver him to the king alive or dead. Under the stimulus of this ban, several plots were laid against the Prince's life: one nearly successful attempt was made in 1582; the last was made in 1584, when he was shot dead at Delft by a man named Balthasar Gérard. The assassin had been moved both by Philip's ban, and by the desire to rid the world of a dangerous heretic: and both Alexander Farnése and representatives of the Church were privy to his plot. He was tortured to death for the deed; but his surviving relatives were richly rewarded by Philip with a patent of nobility and a large gift of landed property.

There can be no doubt that Philip was privy to several attempts to poison or assassinate Queen Elizabeth. On the other hand, he disapproved of the proposal, as part of the Babington plot, to include Lord Burghley among the victims. Others against whom murder-plots were with Philip's authority or approval contrived during the latter years to his reign were Maurice of Nassau (William's son), John of Oldenbarneveld, St. Aldegonde, and King Henry IV of France.

How, then, in the face of this mass of mingled evidence and rumour, are we to sum up Philip's record as an assassin? It must, I think, be granted that comparatively few politicians of that period would

have held that under no conceivable circumstances was it ever permissible to plot the death, by guile, of a harmful individual, whose misdeeds could not otherwise be curbed. But that is not to say that assassination was a widely approved or generally recognized method of exerting political pressure. So far as the general sentiment is concerned, it was held in reserve as a last resort, the use of which could be justified only once in a way, if at all. Only so could the moral stigma, which always in some measure clung to it, be risked or tolerated. What seems to be peculiar about Philip, and is moreover completely consistent with the ethical tone which normally characterized his political behaviour, is that he seems to have imposed on himself very little moral check in the use of this unlovely instrument of kingcraft. The man who could allow the unstinted bloodshed committed by Alva, and who withstood all the Emperor's efforts to hasten its end, would not be likely to have any qualms about secretly contriving the death of any individual obnoxious to him as a Catholic and a Hapsburg: and the evidence, as we have seen, amply warrants us in drawing this inference.

The duty of speaking the truth and keeping one's word — like the duty of having respect unto one's neighbour's life — is one that is imposed alike by secular ethics and by the dictates of the Christian religion. But here again man, and particularly man *quâ* political ruler, has become accustomed to allow himself a margin — more or less liberal — of exceptions. He has not always realized that the practice of lying, in politics as elsewhere, since its object is always that the lie may be believed, is one that is apt to become useless after the first few occasions of employing it; for sooner or later the existence of the practice becomes known, and thereupon men's willingness to believe disappears. The expediency of the moment, however, is usually so clamant, and man's foresightedness is usually so limited, that the self-defeating character of mendacity, not to mention its moral obliquity, has been unable to prevent men from more or less frequently resorting to it. Duplicity and dissimulation have been normal practices on the part of many rulers and their agents; and during our period as well as during others, even solemn treaties were commonly understood to be binding only as long as no tangible advantage seemed to be obtainable by breaking them.

Thus it was that European sovereigns of the sixteenth century and the agents charged with negotiating their affairs did not shrink from the occasional use of falsehood. Henry IV of France and Elizabeth of England (whose mouth, says Dr. Walsh was "apt for lies") were no exceptions. Of William of Orange's alleged duplicity we shall speak later.

Yet there is lying and lying, just as there is homicide and homicide. Clearly, there can be great differences between one lie and another, in regard to (*a*) barefacedness, (*b*) frequency, and (*c*) provocation by circumstance. There are many ways of keeping confidential facts unknown to others, besides mendaciously and explicitly denying them. It is one thing to lie or dissimulate once a year; another to do so every week or every day. It is one thing to lie or dissimulate when one is in an exceptionally tight corner; another, to do so when there is really nothing to be gained by it. Moreover, a general loyalty to truthfulness and to one's pledged word is to be found in many individuals even in an age when dishonesty is very rife. And for all their shortsightedness, men and even politicians are often aware that honesty is the best policy. Whatever may have been the personal practice of William of Orange, for instance, it may safely be said that the Dutch were, on the whole, far more truthful and straightforward in their diplomacy than were the Spanish and Italians.

Now in this matter of mendacity and promise-breaking, as in the last-discussed question of assassination, Philip stands out, amid a galaxy of politicians of whom few or none were wholly innocent, as indulging in the evil practice more frequently and more willingly than did they. It was not that in the abstract — and concretely, in the case of the conduct of his fellow-men — he did not realize the value and claims of truthfulness and good faith. Dr. Walsh quotes him as writing thus to Don John in 1568: "Truth in speaking and fulfilment of promises are the foundation of credit and esteem among men, and that upon which the common intercourse and confidence are based. *This is even more necessary in men of high rank and those who fill great public positions, for on their truth and good faith depend the public faith and security.* I urge it upon you most earnestly, that in this you take great care and heed, that it be well known and understood in all places and seasons that full reliance may be and ought to be placed on whatever you say. . . ." (italics mine.) What could be finer than such counsel? Any insincerity or untruthfulness in his friends and ministers Philip rebuked with the utmost severity. He "hated lies and liars."

Yet when we examine his own conduct, we find him more or less habitually speaking and writing untruthfully and failing to keep his word. Thus, when he left his wife Mary Tudor at the end of August 1555, he promised her, in response to her urgent petition, to return within a month, "though to his own Spanish confidants he said that if once he set foot in Spain again, he would never leave it on so poor an occasion." In December, he sent her a promise that he would come at once — a promise which he repeated a little later. He actually came back to England in March, 1557, and left it for the last time in the following July. During 1558, when Mary's health was failing, "Philip sent her affectionate messages, and promised repeatedly to visit her; but he never did. It is not quite clear how much sincerity there was in his promises. It would seem that he could have managed to get across the channel for a few days at least, had he really desired to do so; . . ."

While concluding the Truce of Vaucelles with France in February, 1556, and impressing the French king with his sincerity, Philip was demanding from Mary that England should join him in a war against France. "Perhaps," says Dr. Walsh, "the French king should have praised Philip's precocious powers of dissimulation instead of his sincerity." In the spring of 1559, he instructed Feria, his ambassador in England, to supply the leading Catholics there with money surreptitiously, and to speak the Protestants fair, so as to put them off their guard and prevent them from appealing to France. While toying with the idea of invading England, he wrote a conciliatory letter which Feria could show to Elizabeth. On leaving the Netherlands in August, 1559, he promised to withdraw the Spanish troops from that country within three or four months: he did not do so; and such was the hostility which their presence aroused that in January, 1516, Granvelle and the Regent deported them to Spain without his orders. As has been pointed out above, his whole policy in the government of the Netherlands involved the violation of his twice-sworn oath to respect the charters and liberties of the country. In 1562 he definitely advised Granvelle to dissimulate in the face of his enemies and accusers. In 1564, when he had at last come to the conclusion that Granvelle must be removed, he engineered his retirement by means of an elaborate system of false pretences, in order to avoid giving the impression that a concession was being made to popular clamour. When forced, by the violence of local feeling in 1566, to grant pardon and toleration in the Netherlands, to withdraw the Inquisition, and to suspend the placards, he formally but privately declared in writing that this pardon was granted only under duresse and that he would not therefore be bound by it; and he informed the pope that his withdrawal of the Inquisition was a mere form of words. This was the year before he sent Alva into the country with an army. He gave it out that he intended to visit the Netherlands himself, and that Alva was simply going to prepare the way for him: but he never went, and in all probability never intended to go. In 1568 he wrote to the pope what Dr. Walsh himself describes as an "obviously insincere letter" about his son Don Carlos. The Marquis of Berghen and the Baron of Montigny came to Spain in 1566 in order to negotiate with Philip, and were received with cordiality: but neither of them was ever allowed to return. The former died in Madrid. The latter was put off with deceitful excuses, was eventually imprisoned, and, after being in his absence sentenced to death by Alva at Brussels, was by Philip's orders secretly strangled in October, 1570, his death being publicly declared to be the result of fever. Not only did Philip rejoice over the massacre of the Huguenots in France in 1572, but he spoke appreciatively of the "long dissimulation" practised in connexion with it. In 1575 he repudiated his debts. He dissimulated with his bastard brother Don John and the latter's secretary Escovedo (1576–1578). In 1578 he agreed to pay the 600 Italian mercenaries whom the pope was sending to Ireland, "but wanted the fact kept secret, in order to avoid offending Queen Elizabeth." He instructed Mendoza to bribe the English ministers.

Along with the deceitfulness of the king went necessarily the deceitfulness of his agents. The Duke of Alva advised his sovereign to dissemble temporarily until he should be strong enough to behead the troublesome nobles of the Low Countries. Alva himself effected the arrest of Counts Egmont and Hoorn only after allaying their suspicions by a hypocritical display of kindness. In 1572 he was encouraging Philip to temporize with England pending the conquest of the Netherlands, so that he could deal with England at his discretion later. But perhaps the most extraordinary example of diplomatic deceitfulness practised conjointly by Philip and one of his agents was one which went near to bringing England into complete subjection

to Spain. For approximately two years
before the Armada sailed, the Duke of
Parma was, with Philip's full knowledge
and consent, carrying on a series of elaborate peace-negotiations with England, for
the sole purpose of deluding Elizabeth,
convincing her of Philip's friendliness, putting her off her guard, and so gaining
time for the preparation of the already full
intended Spanish invasion. On the side
of the Queen, her representatives, and
most of her ministers, the consultations
were sincere, subject to the usual margin
of secretiveness and camouflage incidental
to the diplomacy of that period; and a
genuine desire and hope of coming to
terms was felt. On the Spanish side, the
whole affair from beginning to end was a
protracted piece of hypocrisy and lying, a
mere "ruse de guerre." While it was in
progress, similar but less elaborate deceit
was practised on France, in order that she
might be kept occupied with her own
internal broils, might rest confidently on
Philip's untruthfully professed friendship,
and so not go to England's help. Similar
duplicity continued to mark the Spanish
diplomatic relations with France, even after
the death of Henry III in 1589. At least
one further attempt was made on England
under the mask of indirect assurances of
Spanish friendship. When, after years of
magnificent service, Parma at last incurred
the suspicion and jealousy of his royal
master, the latter masked his real sentiments and intentions by means of a series
of flattering lies. Parma's death in December, 1592, put him beyond Philip's power
to wrong him further. In 1596, the king
again repudiated his debts.

Surely we have here a life-long practice
of falsehood and deceit far exceeding that
more or less normal secretiveness and lack
of candour which is apt to mark all diplomacy, and which certainly characterizes
much of the intercourse between European
states in the sixteenth century. Up to a
point, I suppose one may say, it was so
common that it deceived nobody. But
Philip's record shows a love of "by-paths

and indirect crook'd ways" which puts the
deceitfulness of his contemporaries completely in the shade. We may or may not
wish to make our own Motley's strong
characterization of Philip as "the great
father of lies who sat in the Escorial": but,
rhetoric apart, the phrase is not substan-
tially incorrect. Dr. Walsh does not use
such strong language about it: but what
else in substance is conveyed by his repeated allusions to Philip's masterly dissimulation? Mr. G. Edmundson says of
him: "He had great belief in his powers
of tortuous diplomacy; and, instead of taking the prompt measures which are essential in a crisis, he sat brooding in his cabinet at Segovia, and slowly evolving by
what course of action he could best circum-
vent his difficulties, cajole his adversaries,
and, it may be added, deceive his friends."

No one will deny that his frequent recourse to mendacity and deceit was practised in the steady pursuit of a dominating
ambition or, let us say, two dominating
ambitions — to enhance his own royal
power, and to defend Catholicism. But of
the fact that he did actually and habitually
practise deceit the record of his doings,
even as his panegyrist presents it, leaves
not the slightest room for doubt. Dr.
Walsh, therefore, stultifies his own narrative, when he writes of Philip: "His mag-
nanimity and Christian charity make a
contrast with the duplicity of Henry and
with the cold calculating malice of the
Cecils. . . ." With the story of the long-
drawn-out peace negotiations preceding the
Armada before our eyes, we deem this
author to be but playing with facts when
he writes: "Philip . . . suffered . . . from
another kind of blindness from which
Elizabeth was singularly free: with an almost childish trust, he was constantly
under-estimating his enemies and their
power to do him harm. In this he was
anything but Machiavellian. . . ." The
names of the two sovereigns need rather
to be interchanged here — at least if regard is to be had to the diplomatic episode
to which I allude. Dr. Walsh's reviewer

in *The Times Literary Supplement* for February 19, 1938, is as inaccurate as Dr. Walsh himself. "Certainly by contrast with the widespread opportunism and duplicity of his time," he writes, "Philip II's character stands out nobly. It had extraordinary consistency." But consistency in ambition is by no means incongruous with opportunism and duplicity. As regards these latter, Philip appears, not better, but consistently worse, than most of his contemporaries. Nor can I at all understand how a scientific historian like Mr. Trevor Davies, aiming to "steer an even . . . course between the Scylla of Protestant, Liberal, and Anti-clerical prepossessions and the Charybdis of Roman Catholic partisanship," can bring himself to write of Philip: "Duplicity and even crime are possibly, though by no means certainly, to be found as incidents in his diplomatic and political life; but such things were no part of his normal behaviour. Those who knew him best recognised him as truthful, . . ."

It is no easy task to sum up the evidence for Philip's character with justice and accuracy, even when we remember that our business is to describe the character, and not to acquit or convict the man, and also that a monarch has sharper ethical problems to face than those which challenge ordinary humanity. There is in Philip's case a further fact to be reckoned with, to which allusion has not yet been made. His family was tainted with insanity. The cause of this was probably the chronic inbreeding which marked its matrimonial history. Philip's grandmother died at the age of seventy-six, after having been hopelessly mad for fifty years. The epileptic

Don Carlos, son of Philip and his first cousin, was as degenerate in mind and character, as he was obviously misshapen in body. Philip's successors on the Spanish throne exhibited both physically and mentally the abnormalities of their heritage. Philip himself was the child of first cousins. His mother was the offspring of several generations of consanguineous marriages, and her two younger sons died in early childhood of epilepsy. How far he himself may have been affected by the taint it is impossible to say, even though his normal thinking powers never betrayed any signs of it.

No doubt his modern apologists are right in insisting that the detestation in which he was long held in Protestant countries engendered a traditional view of him which did less than justice to his piety and his private virtues. But the traditional horror felt towards him is not necessarily on that account to be regarded as groundless, or as due simply to religious narrowmindedness. The unrestricted and extensive use which he made of falsehood and bloodshed in order, not only to serve the Roman Church, but also to defend and increase the glory of his throne and dynasty, though not inconsistent with earnest religiousness and with certain personal graces, naturally and inevitably blackened his reputation, and amply explains and goes far to justify the opinions customarily entertained regarding him. It is no Protestant fanatic, but so sympathetic an historian as Mr. Edward Armstrong, who writes: "Given the character of Philip II, the personal union of Spain and the Netherlands was an unmixed evil, . . ."

TWO TWENTIETH-CENTURY SPANISH VIEWS

Elegy to Philip II

ANTONIO BALLESTEROS Y BERETTA

Few Spanish historians of the twentieth century have enjoyed a wider reputation than Antonio Ballesteros y Beretta (1880–1941). His encyclopedic nine-volume *Historia de España y su influencia en la historia universal* stands as a monument to his organizational ability and indefatigability as an historian. Educated in Spain, he studied both letters and law and turned ultimately to history as his life work. Widely recognized for his endeavors in this field, Ballesteros served for a time with the High Council of Scientific Investigations in Spain and received both the Grand Cross of Isabelle and the Grand Cross of Naval Merit for his services. The selection included in this volume comes from a group of sketches written by Ballesteros on significant figures in Spanish history. A sample of his musings on Philip II, it represents Ballesteros' attempt to explain Philip's international policies and to relate them to his personality and to his advisers. The myriad of characters introduced into this sketch implement Ballesteros' view that Philip was strongly influenced by his advisers. He also compares the Prudent King with his counterparts in England, France, and the Low Countries and comes to the conclusion that he was more upright and high-minded than his contemporaries in Europe.

PHILIP began his political apprenticeship quite young; he was fifteen when his father assigned him administrative duties. In 1543, he married his cousin, Princess María of Portugal. Since the Emperor (Charles V) favored a new tie with the Portuguese dynasty, the marriage fulfilled both the political interests of Spain and the emotional needs of the young prince.

Especially at the beginning of his reign, Philip II's political policies were those of his father, who was guided in his time by the wise counsel of his grandfather, the Catholic King (Ferdinand). There are two significant documents which contain the political principles and recommendations passed down by Charles to his son Philip. Both documents were written by Charles in Palamos on May 4 and 5, 1543, on the eve of his last trip to Germany. Secret instructions, they have revealed to posterity the exceptional talents of their author, who, if there was no other evidence than these two documents, would be adjudged a great, unmatched statesman.

A widower after only two short years of marriage, at his father's request Philip went to Flanders in 1548, a time decisive in the life of the Prince. Philip visited the cities of Genoa, Milan, and Mantua, and rode on horseback through the Tyrol, Bavaria, and Alsace, arriving in Flanders in 1549. After spending some months in the Low Countries, he accompanied the Emperor to Germany.

The chronicles have described the long talks Charles V had with his son and his advice to Philip on policies which the

From Antonio Ballesteros y Beretta, *Figuras imperiales: Alfonso VII, el Emperador, Colon, Fernando el Católico, Carlos V, Felipe II* (Buenos Aires, 1947), pp. 72–92. Reprinted by permission of Espasa-Callpa, S.A., Madrid, and the son of the author. [Editors' Translation.]

prince ought diligently to pursue. In these years the Prince was a faithful disciple of the Emperor. Circumspect, solemn, quiet, young Philip was a living image of his father, and like the Emperor he followed the advice of Chievres without deviating at all from established policies. Likewise Philip blindly obeyed the dictates of his father, a fact essential for understanding the first years of his reign.

At the age of thirty the Emperor had shed his serious, melancholy air, but Philip kept his seriousness, inherited from his Portuguese mother, all his life. Philip's demeanor was such that if there seemed to be a great deal of the Spanish knight in him, there was also the extreme aloofness of the Lusitanian nobleman.

In 1550, Philip returned to Spain, and within three years Charles arranged an English wedding for his son, a diplomatic coup that crowned the political career of the Emperor. Philip II married Mary of England, but hardly for love. The queen was thirty-eight, her suitor barely twenty-six. In addition a long, difficult spinsterhood had robbed this Tudor of her charm and physical attractiveness, which according to the chronicles, she possessed in her early youth.

France was Charles' principal preoccupation. With the wedding of his son (to Mary), he realized his golden dream, the encirclement of the French nation, the surrounding of the House of Valois, the rivals of the Hapsburgs. To the east was Germany; to the north Flanders; to the south Spain and loyal Italy; and with England to the west on the northern side of France, the French state could not expand without eminent danger to its existence as a nation. Events soon confirmed the foresight of Charles V.

The Emperor abdicated in 1555 and retired to Yuste, directing the world from his monastic cell there. French violation of the Truce of Vaucelles (February 15, 1556) caused the rupture with Spain hoped for by Pope Paul IV and his nephews, the Caraffa, who supported the Guise family,

influential in the councils of Henry II (king of France). The head of the Guise family, Francis, who had stopped Charles V at Metz, demanded the Kingdom of Naples which set off war. Philip II went from Flanders to London in order to get the aid of his wife Mary Tudor. The queen consort agreed to help, and the campaign began, ending finally with the glorious Spanish victory at San Quentin.

In Europe, however, the political situation was in flux. Events and individuals were interacting to set off an ideological revolution. Philip lost his father and adviser; Mary Tudor died and left the King of Spain to solve the problems of state for himself. But what had happened besides this to produce the change? The secret lay with France, which had been the enemy of Spain for over one hundred years. At this time France wanted friendship, seemingly a sincere and lasting friendship. The king of Spain desired it, and essentially the Guises in France desired it also. With religious ferment going on all about them, two prelates, the Bishop of Arras, Antonio Perrenot de Granvela (representing Spain), and the Cardinal of Lorraine (representing France), one of the Guises, met at Cercamps to bring the two warring nations together. At bottom, the agreement they made was a matter of internal politics. The Catholic Guises detested the Chatillon, protectors of the French Protestants, and for these two factions the internal struggle was just beginning. Tired of war, Spain and Philip II were gladly willing to accept a peace which seemed advantageous from their point of view. As a symbol of the new alliance, Elizabeth of Valois arrived in Spain to become the new Spanish queen. In this matter, Philip II was following the wishes of his father, who had advised his marriage to a French princess.

At this time the French monarchy was not a force in European politics, and the prestige and power of Spain were growing in Europe. With political foresight Charles had accurately judged the outcome of the encirclement of France. Still, despite the internal struggles which rent that country, it managed to survive, principally because of the political talents of one woman, Catherine de Medici. Treacherous and two-faced, she used diplomacy which attempted, but failed, to deceive Philip II.

Having a suspicious nature, the king did not trust the Guises: their friendship was still new and as yet untried. However, the convenience of the alliance kept the Guises loyal and faithful to Spain. Opposing the Guises in France was Montmorency, the Fabio Cunctator, who had been defeated at San Quentin. Despite being a Catholic, he allied himself with his Protestant nephews, the Chatillons. Later he did a turnabout and fought against the Protestants; but he never once favored a Spanish alliance.

Of Philip II's many enemies, we shall highlight two, whose great power and wily feminine ways made them greatly to be feared. We are referring to Elizabeth of England and Catherine de Medici. These two women, beset by misfortune before assuming their thrones, underwent unhappy experiences in their youth that embittered them, but prepared them for a life of continuous intrigue.

In prison much of the time, poorly clothed, and ill-fed, Elizabeth passed her youth constantly fearing for her life, haunted by the memory of the insatiable lust of her father (Henry VIII) and of the scaffold where her mother Anne Boleyn met her death. For many, Philip II's kindness to Elizabeth I has been an inexplicable mystery; rumors were always current that the Spanish prince and the persecuted Elizabeth held secret meetings that aroused the jealousy of Mary Tudor. What is more, Philip went so far as to save the life of Elizabeth, his future enemy. Today the reasons for the king protecting Elizabeth are obvious. It could be argued that Charles V advised him to do it, but in this case Philip took account of the international situation on his own. If the Anglican Elizabeth should die like Jane Grey, and if Mary Tudor had no offspring, the heiress

to the English throne would inevitably be Mary Stuart, who was married to the heir to the French throne and would therefore become the future queen of France. Besides, Mary Stuart was the daughter of Mary of Lorraine, a niece of the Duke of Guise, who was at that time an arch-enemy of Spain. This then explains why Philip preferred to protect Elizabeth: he wished to prevent the union of England, Scotland, and France under one monarch, a union obviously detrimental to the House of Hapsburg, which would be the first to suffer from an expanded House of Valois.

Soon after the accession of Elizabeth, Philip II asked for her hand in marriage. The queen did not refuse the proposal outright but began a coy flirtation of the kind she carried on with so many princes. When she heard of Philip's marriage to Elizabeth of Valois, she informed the Spanish ambassador that the king had found a wife elsewhere because she had not given him a definite answer.

At the age of eleven Catherine de Medici was humiliated by the people of Florence. In a revolt against her family, the Florentines had kidnapped her from the convent where she was receiving her education. For a time these same rebels pondered setting Catherine up on the city walls as a target for the cannon of the Medici and of imprisoning her with the rest of the courtesans. Later when she married the French prince, she suffered further humiliation when she had to seek aid from her husband's mistresses, among them the all-powerful Diane de Poitiers, favorite of Henry II, who had relegated his legitimate wife to an inferior position. Catherine thus became a bitter, vengeful woman; that attribute, coupled with the devious and unscrupulous methods that she was forced to adopt for survival in her youth, were later used with dynastic fervor in favor of her children. History has recognized her undisputed talents as valuable political weapons; indeed, her practices were models of treachery and dissimulation, common to the Florentine environment, but far surpassing the teachings of her countryman, Niccolo Machiavelli.

Legend tells us about deadly perfumed gloves, of slow-working poisons, of the devious arts and potions, created in the shadows of hidden rooms by Ruggiere, whose tower still exists. In the Castle at Blois are the closets where Catherine kept her strange concoctions. Whether all this is fact or fancy makes little difference, for other significant factors made Philip II's mother-in-law a formidable enemy. In the dispatches directed to her ambassadors, she was able to spread the honey of false affection and to appear as a kind and loving mother, but this only concealed her craftiness and deceitfulness.

Francis II was the first son of Catherine de Medici to rule France. A young man, he was intrigued by the beauty of Mary Stuart. Philip II distrusted him, principally because he was dominated by the Guises. When Francis died within a year, Catherine became the power behind the throne as regent of Charles IX; but with her in power, Philip no longer had to fear a French royal alliance with the Guises. With Catholics opposing Protestants in France, Philip's sympathies naturally lay on the Catholic side. In an attempt to stop the spread of Calvinism, he thus saw fit to help the Guises, but he preferred secret, clandestine aid rather than open, official relationships. Up-to-date espionage reports kept him informed of what was happening in the neighboring French monarchy and helped the Spanish ruler to achieve diplomatic victories. One prestigious Catholic leader, the Gascon Balaise de Montluc, author of extremely interesting memoirs, came to Philip II during this period asking him to save the Catholic cause in France, which, he felt, was virtually bleeding to death.

In order to judge the ensuing events dispassionately, it is essential to make some fundamental observations. Protestantism arose at the time of Charles V, and the Reformation was a stormy enough force to check the power of the Emperor. This religious movement reached its peak at the time of Philip II, dividing Europe into two apparently irreconciliable camps. As defender of the Catholic cause, Charles V had struggled against the Lutherans, while Philip II had to fight the Calvinists. The Lutherans however, were more doctrinal than combative and would fight only when it was necessary. The Calvinists, on the other hand, were more militant and aggressive and fought with the fury of madmen seeking the destruction of their adversaries.

Unintentionally, perhaps, the Calvinists became the great ideological adversaries of Philip II, for it was the Huguenots of France and the Flemish rebels who enthusiastically followed the precepts of the Prophet from Geneva. For his part the King of Spain simply could not allow the existence of heresy in either area. The hegemony of the House of Hapsburg was dependent upon his leadership. The monarch of the most Catholic of Catholic states was obliged to be the champion of the Counter Reformation, a fact which explains the entire reign of Philip II. Let us see why.

With its elegant, pagan spirit, the Renaissance was a tolerant age. This is evidenced by the Epicurean phrase of Leo X upon judging the first sparks of the Reformation: *"Sono invidie fratesche."* Charles V, a man of the Renaissance and a child of his time, had shown his willingness to temporize with the Lutheranism of his princes, and only when he saw his political authority in danger, did he resort to force. Philip II, paladin of the Counter Reformation, tried to impose the precepts of the Council of Trent on all Europe, and was tolerant only in the manner of the Guises, Mary Tudor, and Elizabeth of England.

In the sixteenth century the European world was in a critical period. In the political order crises were acute, especially in regard to the old concept of nationalism. This feudal ideal, which identified the nation with the king, had survived; to be loyal to the nation was to be loyal to the king.

But a new belief grew up to challenge and weaken this older ideal, and almost to destroy it, although absolutism lasted until the time of the French Revolution. This belief was freedom of conscience. At first Lutherans and Calvinists tried to make obedience to royal power compatible with their dedication to freedom of conscience, but the kings strongly resisted granting the confessional freedom favored by the Protestants. In fact the monarchs engaged in terrible purges, which ultimately set off a series of violent religious wars. These put at odds the old ideal of a subject's duty to his sovereign and the new ideal of freedom of conscience. In order to secure this right, they (the Lutherans and Calvinists) ultimately found it necessary to fight against their king.

It is now time to introduce an avowed enemy of Philip II. As a French nationalist, Coligny hated the dominance of Spain; as a Calvinist he detested the unquestioned leader of Catholic Europe. A noble, austere, ingenuous person, Gaspar de Coligny fought bravely against the enemies of France. Coligny's father, Gaspar de Chatillon, Marshal of Chatillon, lost a portion of his possessions in the Franche-Comté to the Spaniards during the time of Charles V. As a compensation, the French king gave Chatillon the principality of Orange. This was a strange coincidence, since later the admiral's son-in-law (Coligny) would be the famous William of Orange. Chatillon's brothers opposed the growing power of the Guises. The second-born, Gaspar, was an admiral; the third-born, Francis d'Andelot, followed in Gaspar's every step, leading a contemporary authority to call him the "shadow." Odet, the oldest of the Chatillon, was a cardinal from infancy and an abominable example for a cardinal of the Roman church: he protected Calvinism. In addition, the Chatillon counted on their side, their uncle, the old constable Anne Montmorency.

The Flemish question now facing us is generally judged on an emotional basis. For Philip II the Low Countries were a political bastion, the most strategic in all the Spanish Empire. From Flanders he watched and directed the House of Hapsburg in Germany. As leader of the Hapsburgs he needed the Low Countries, whose industrial and mercantile vigor made it a bountiful land. The Low Countries had provided the Hapsburg Emperor with more resources for his wars than all the other provinces of his immense dominions combined. Moreover, the Low Countries were strategically located near the vulnerable borders of France, the traditional enemy of the Hapsburgs. It may be remembered that during the First World War Germany attacked France through Belgium, for from there it was possible to attack Great Britain. It is only necessary to recall Napoleon's famous phrase: "Amberes will always be a loaded pistol aimed at the heart of England." Philip II intervened militarily in France from Flanders; Don Juan of Austria, while in the Low Countries, dreamed of saving Mary Stuart in order to make her his wife; and plans for the Great Armada called for the forces of Alexander Farnése to go from Flanders to England.

Before proceeding it is also essential to explain the political theory which grew out of the Renaissance, which was deeply rooted in European attitudes. Such an explanation is necessary in order to present a balanced account. Philip II, like his contemporary rulers, supported the theory of absolutism: the will of the monarch was law and royal authority must be preserved at all costs. This feeling was shared equally by Elizabeth Tudor, Catherine de Medici, and Philip II. Any means were considered acceptable in dealing with the rebel who committed the crime of lèse-majesté (offending the king). This explains the terrible intolerance of Philip II toward the Flemish rebels, especially in his attitude toward the Prince of Orange. The latter boasted of knowing the personal whims of the sovereign, but it was not precisely that.

Wiser, and a better politician than his contemporaries, Orange knew and recognized absolutist theories of government.

Philip ruled Flanders through Margaret of Parma, and we say that he ruled through her, because the king's correspondence shows that Margaret was an instrument of her brother, whose orders she executed without hesitation. Even in emergencies, she found it necessary to wait for orders from Madrid, orders which were always late because of the great distance they had to come and the irresolution of the king.

Much has been written about the irresolute character of the monarch, and perhaps we shall find the explanation for it in a fact which historians have not discussed. One of the most absolute kings in history, he, nevertheless, almost never adopted his own ideas; and in spite of his penchant for one-man rule, he put very little of himself into his major decisions. Charles V, more ductile, tolerant, and amiable exercised true personal power and gave every act his personal seal of approval. Is it because Philip did not have any of his own ideas? In reply, I do not doubt that in most cases he did not have them, because he could not have them. He was very discreet, and he knew that probably those ideas that did occur to him were not sound.

He lacked certain elements of good judgment. Charles V was a constant traveller. Educated in Flanders, he knew French and Flemish perfectly and learned to speak Spanish, German, and Italian, and lived for a long time in the European countries that constituted his Empire. He knew their customs and psychology; thus he made decisions speedily. Charles V did not need advisors to tell him the meaning of his subjects' actions or their wishes and aspirations. How different was Philip II's situation. A Spaniard with all the Spanish virtues, he scarcely understood French and Italian, which he did not speak. At times he even had to have French letters translated for him. In addition he was not acquainted with the habits of those living outside the Iberian peninsula, and it was essential for him to compensate for this lack of knowledge. Thus he had Councils. Disoriented, Philip II needed information. He could not make decisions personally as his father had done but had to wait for the opinions and advice of others. This was one of the reasons for his inexplicable delays.

Granvelle was one of the advisors he most often consulted. The Archbishop of Malina (Granvelle) was opposed to the calling of the Estates General in the Low Countries; thus Philip did not convoke it for many years. Granvelle suspected de Montigny and the Marquis of Berghes and branded them as dangerous; the king remembered this opinion later on. In the Low Countries Granvelle recommended the use of force; he firmly supported the appointment of the Duke of Alba; he suggested the construction of citadels in towns in order to subdue the rebels, and inspired Philip's sternest measures. He instigated the kidnapping of the Count of Buren, son of the Silent One (William the Silent), and his advice also resulted in the proscription against William of Orange.

Philip, however, took suggestions from others of lower standing than this illustrious counselor. During the first stages of the Dutch revolt, Philip listened to Father Lorenzo de Villavincencio, a fact revealed by Gachard, and to the accountant, Alonso del Canto, the one an Andalusian cleric and the other a Segovian from Santa María de Nieva. Both acted as his spies, and if one treats them sympathetically, he would be able to say this of them: they were carried away by their own prejudices, presenting rumor as actual fact and fostering Philip's intransigence toward the Flemish. The spirit of the king was thus predisposed toward a repressive policy that foreshadowed the bloody era of the Duke of Alba.

Don Fernando Alvárez de Toledo, third Duke of Alba, who was a model of loyalty to the crown and a fervent Catholic, has been considered as the archetype of Spanish intransigence. He was described by his contemporaries as tall and thin and intense.

Let us point out that Philip II was by

no means an exception in using repressive methods. We need only to recall the persecutions ordered by Elizabeth of England, the tortures in the tower of London, and the horrible night in Paris, when the Huguenots were bathed in blood. We must insist again upon this fact: to the absolute monarch, the rebel was an outlaw. When the Flemish appealed to the English queen for official backing, she refused to help them, and if she did, indeed, aid them secretly, she denied them open support because she found it repugnant to deal with rebels.

Alba fulfilled his mission and re-established royal power. It is not true that all Europe was horrified at Alba's policies. Catherine de Medici congratulated the king on the triumphs of the Duke of Alba, and the English queen was not at all moved by his executions to which she had become accustomed.

From the military point of view, Alba's campaigns deserved only praise from the experts, for without a doubt he was the best general of his day. Having subdued the Low Countries, however, he had the arrogance of the victor that combined with his financial policies to bring about the rebellion of 1572. This began a merciless war that lasted over twenty years and that resulted finally in the independence of the Northern States (the Netherlands). Alba's tenth-penny and twentieth-penny taxes irritated both Catholics and Protestants and were ruinous to the country, which preferred to revolt rather than to die of hunger. Responsibility for these events lies exclusively with the Duke of Alba, for the king, in a letter of February (1572) had stated that he must "treat them (the Dutch) with consideration, which is the substance and essence of statecraft." The president of the Council of Castile, Diego Covarrubias, bishop of Segovia, and Dr. Andres Pons, both disapproved of the Duke of Alba's fiscal policies, which they considered unwise.

This same crucial year (1572) the French intervened in Flanders. Admiral Coligny, a bitter enemy of Spain and now reconciled with the French royal house, obtained approval from that tortured and troubled monarch, Charles IX, for his war plans against Philip II. This time, however, the politics of the de Medici, bound to those of the Guise because of fear of Huguenot domination, saved Spain from a dangerous assault. She (Catherine de Medici) convinced her son to instigate that deed known as the Massacre of the Eve of Saint Bartholomew's Day (August 24, 1572). Coligny died, and with him was lost the only Frenchman capable of fighting against the power of Philip II. Since 1568 a secret alliance had existed between Coligny and the Prince of Orange for the purpose of securing freedom of conscience. Catherine de Medici and Charles IX, in the meantime, pursued a two-faced policy, preserving on the surface an official friendship with the Spanish king while secretly encouraging upheaval in the Low Countries.

We have mentioned before that the Prince of Orange, William of Nassau, was a person of immense importance in the rebellion in the Low Countries and became the focus of the uprising against Philip II. The aims of this powerful enemy of Spain are not clear. Orange, a Catholic prince, perhaps because of its advantages for him, was then leaning toward Lutheranism and at this time demonstrated an intolerant opposition toward Calvinism. In reality he was a Cassandrian opportunist, a supporter of religious toleration, at bottom a deist, but not, perhaps, attached to any particular religious faith. His expansive and garrulous nature contrasted sharply with his tight-lipped reserve on political questions that earned him the title, *the Silent*.

Orange compromised with his peers because he believed it otherwise impossible to succeed in a rebellion against the invincible might of Spain. Later on he took advantage of his opportunities in such a skillful way, that even in our own day, we cannot categorically state that he was motivated by excessive ambition or by ungenerous aims. Furthermore, for a long time he proclaimed the sovereignty of the Spanish monarch while fighting against his armies. In these acts there appears a kind of patriotic altruism, recognized by the Duke of Alenço or the Archduke Matias. At this juncture William seemed too disinterested; his own personal interests seemed secondary. However, there is reason to suspect that one of his great political talents was to wait patiently for the opportune moment. He realized that excessive impatience might prevent his ultimate success. That incipient state (the Netherlands) needed the resources that more powerful nations could provide, and this was the basis of his diplomacy, which courted the French and English. Probably this astute, cautious Prince had no strict religious beliefs. In his second marriage to Anne of Saxony he submitted to all kinds of conjugal humiliations in order to obtain the aid of the German princes. Later he felt that French help would be useful; he thus divorced Anne and married Charlotte of Bourbon, an ex-nun and ardent Calvinist. Still later he arranged another marriage with Coligny's daughter, joining in this manner two families very strongly opposed to Philip II.

In 1573 the Spanish king changed his policy in Flanders. Those writers who have accused the hermit of the Escorial of always practicing a policy of repression have not seen fit to remember the benevolent rule of Don Luis de Resquesens, knight commander of Castile. During this period Philip II was also guided by the advice of one who had witnessed Flemish events first hand and who had lived in the Low Countries for a long time. This authority, who carried on an active correspondence with the king, was the great scripturist, Arias Montaño. Generous and wise, Montaño was a renowned humanist, who compared the Low Countries and the healthy optimism of its inhabitants to the classical provinces of Hellas and to the simple customs of the people of ancient Greece. An advocate of benevolent policies and proponent of a general pardon for all rebels,

Montaño had four conferences of three hours each with the new governor (Resquens). Montaño's influence has been brought out in a well-conceived book by Morales Oliver.

The government of de Resquesens meant the end of the reign of terror. Affable, humane, and tolerant in political matters, Resquesens did not, however, compromise, willingly on religious questions. A child of his century, Catholic, and a true Spaniard, he held the same intolerance as the soldiers, whose attitude is reflected in the *Diálogo de los pajes,* written by Diego de Hermosilla, in Calderón's *Sitio de Breda,* and in *Don Quixote.*

The successor to Resquesens, Don Juan of Austria, was the incarnation of a medieval knight, whose historical significance has not as yet been clearly defined. He swept through the Flemish countryside like a gust of wind, a medieval hero who found the last sparks of life stamped out in the cold mists of the North. Looking back, one can easily misconstrue the mistakes of Don Juan of Austria.

During his governorship the northern provinces (the Netherlands) revolted once more against the sovereignty of Philip II; to the south, the Belgian Catholics and the Council of State were behaving in such a way as to appear disloyal to a ruler like Don Juan. If it had not been for the timely arrival of Spanish troops from Italy under Alexander Farnése, the situation might have turned into a disaster for Don Juan, for it was Farnése who saved the hero of Lepanto. Unfortunately for Don Juan's reputation, Farnése's enlightened rule eclipsed the misguided government of the bastard son of Charles V.

Under Farnése the Flemish problem became even more complex and more critical. Now the problem was more than simply a matter of a rebellious people against their legitimate sovereign. In the Low Countries the foreign enemies of Spain had discovered a vulnerable spot in the Spanish Empire, and it was here they conspired against Spain. Although Henry III did not officially authorize the action of the Duke of Alençon, the latter used French troops to fight in the Low Countries in the hope of becoming ruler over the area. The English queen also sent her favorite, the Count of Leicester, to the Netherlands. Even Germany saw the northern territories as possible appendages to the Holy Roman Empire and refused to obey orders from Madrid; this is exemplified by the policy of the inept Archduke Matias.

In 1578 came the imposing figure of Alexander Farnése, the most complete man of his time. He was the quintessence of Spanish wisdom, energy, and solemnity which he combined with Italian ductility, inherited from his father. At the age of thirty-four in the prime of life, he showed exceptional abilities, both as an adroit politician and as an extraordinary military leader. He alone foresaw the only possible solution to the Flemish problem with its labyrinth of conflicting interests and ambitions. He astutely exploited the differences between Waloons and Flemings; he negotiated and waged war skillfully; he was alternately mild and forceful; fortune favored him, and he saved for Spain all that could be saved at that time — the Catholic provinces of the South. For him they were a smaller but more secure patrimony for the Spanish Hapsburgs.

Farnése, however, was not able to realize his goals. The Flemish problem had become increasingly complex and puzzling, especially with the heightening of international tensions, and Philip II had to spend the last twenty years of his reign in continuous fighting. Since men of Farnése's stature were scarce, the king needed the talents of his nephew for other arduous tasks.

In 1580 Philip II achieved the unification of the Iberian peninsula. It was the one real success of his reign. Philip had a Portuguese mother; he was taught by the Portuguese Doña Leonor de Mascarenhas; he spoke Portuguese; and had as his favorite at court, Don Ruy Gómez de Silva, of an ancient Portuguese royal house. The annex-

ation of Portugal thus became one of the most important goals of his reign, the focal point of his diplomacy. It was the only undertaking the monarch carried out quickly, efficiently, and steadfastly. Don Cristobal de Moura skillfully directed the diplomatic negotiations; the old Duke of Alba won his last military victories in the conquest of Portugal; and the Marquis de Santa Cruz defeated the Prior of Crato in the waters of the Atlantic. The annexation of Portugal was, in fact, the high point of Philip II's reign.

The equivocal attitude of Henry III and Catherine de Medici toward the Portuguese affair did not endear the Valois to the Spanish king, but his animosity was directed more toward those who seemed most dangerous, the House of Tudor. A mutual feeling of distrust had grown up between them. While Queen Elizabeth secretly protected the rebellious Flemish, Philip used Spanish treasure to prepare for war against England on the Portugese coast. Philip also encouraged Catholic conspiracies against Elizabeth and attempted to save Mary Stuart, destined by the Virgin Queen for the executioner's blade. All this produced a war crisis. For Philip it appeared necessary to avenge the English insults by preparing a gigantic enterprise calculated to break the power of Great Britain. Farnése had already contemplated the invasion of England; in the eighteenth century the ministers of Charles III and Louis XVI projected a similar scheme; later General Hoche conceived a like enterprise; and from Boulogne, Napoleon laid plans to bring down the English colossus by invading the invulnerable island with his *Grand Army*. But since William the Conqueror, such a landing had been impossible without the complicity of the inhabitants. For Spain the factors contributing to the debacle of the Invincible Armada (1588) were the delays in making preparations, the low state of the treasury, the ineptitude of Medina Sidonia, and English efficiency.

After the battle, although the real crisis had passed, the two rivals (Philip II and

Elizabeth I) still remained face to face. England had emerged victorious but was still on the defensive. It had escaped the blow of the Spanish colossus, but the strength of Spain remained intact. Recovering from the misfortune it suffered, the Spanish nation had more than enough spirit, determination, and energy to rise again vigorously. In 1588, the same year as the defeat, the prudent but dilatory king took aggressive action in France in search of a crown, proof of his ability to recoup. Woe to the enemies of Spain if Philip had been able to finance his program of aggrandizement! After the Armada England vainly attempted to invade the heart of Spain, but its actions at La Coruña, Belén, and Cádiz were only scratches on the giant's skin.

Indeed, the Spanish Empire had expanded greatly. The defection of the northern provinces in the Low Countries meant nothing compared to expansion elsewhere — into the Portuguese eastern dominions, Brazil, the American wilderness, the provinces of El Dorado, and France, where in his last years at the Escorial the ascetic king was lured on by the compelling gleam of the French crown. In Germany the Empire was obedient and subservient to Charles V's first-born. In Italy Spanish power was incontestable; the Lombard, Neapolitan, and Sicilian dominions were the richest in all Italy, and when the pope clashed with Spain on temporal matters, he was put in his proper place by the Spanish monarch. The Duke of Savoy owed his crown to Philip, and out of gratitude and because of blood ties remained loyal to him. Impotent Venice could do little more than vent its anti-Spanish feelings by repeating the piquant gossip of its astute ambassadors. At the same time Spanish garrisons in Tuscany and Genoa kept careful watch over the Medici of Florence. Their bankers had lent money to Philip II at usurious interest and gambled their economic future on the luck and credit of Spain, which hoped to repay these loans with riches taken from the mines of Austria.

On August 1, 1589, Henry III, the effeminate sovereign of the French mignons, died at the hands of the assassin, Jacob Clemente. Henry died without an heir, intensifying the struggle between Catholics and Huguenots. The Protestants had a leader of great capacity and wisdom in Henry of Navarre; the fanatics of the Catholic League (headed by the Guise) found its strength in the people of Paris. For Philip it seemed that friendship with the Guise would finally bear fruit, for the French Catholics seemed ready to offer the throne to Philip II. In the meantime, the Spanish diplomatic triumvirate of Don Bernardino de Mendoza, Juan Bautista de Tassis, and the knight commander, Juan Moreno, contrived to obtain the throne for the Infanta Isabel Clara Eugenia.

The timely military intervention of Farnése (1590 and 1592) had done much to jeopardize the position of the Bearnes (Henry of Navarre), but as a result of his conversion to Catholicism, Henry successfully met this dangerous challenge and subsequently eliminated the Spanish menace (1594). After the Franco-Spanish War (1595-98), the two countries concluded the Peace of Vervins (May 2, 1598), the final stage in the prolonged struggle between the House of Hapsburg and the French house of Valois-Bourbon. Philip also resolved the Flemish problem along the lines suggested by Farnése: he granted the southern provinces as a kingdom to his favorite daughter, the Infanta Isabel Clara Eugenia, and her husband, the Archduke Albert.

It is unwise, oftentimes, to use success as a criterion of judgment. We would thus completely misjudge Philip II and his naval policy, if we judged him solely by the results of the expedition against England. Despite the failure of his planning in this episode, the broad, persevering view of the son of Charles V was one of his principal virtues. Convinced that whoever mastered the sea would master the continent, the monarch attempted to assert Spanish naval supremacy. In addition to the religious motive, the battle against the Turks at Lepanto had as its aim the attainment of Spanish hegemony in the Mediterranean. As Spanish ships had become masters of the interior sea where English warships had not yet reached, so it became absolutely vital for Spain to dominate the Atlantic, where its interest were even more far-reaching.

The conquest of Portugal had completed the coastal dominions of the (Iberian) Peninsula and increased Spanish naval influence. It also made it necessary to prevent the growth of English maritime power that interrupted Spanish communication with America. This was the reason for the Invincible Armada and other such enterprises. It became a deadly duel in which the prize to the victor was predominance in the Atlantic.

Although Philip II understood the Spanish temperament perfectly and fathomed the psychology of his people to such an extent that it was his own, he also had a deep love for America. He was vitally concerned about Spain's position in the Atlantic and about his imperial interests, both those of the indigenes and his Spanish colonial subjects. Because it was something Hispanic, something familiar, Philip felt a special affection for America. His naval policy thus had no other end than to save Spanish America, and thanks to his efforts and concern, the immense Spanish Empire did not suffer serious losses.

Pirates, it is true, threatened the coasts of continental America. The depredations of Hawkins, Cavendish, and the renowned Drake, the *Sea Dragon,* who plundered the rich Antillean ports, occurred one after another. The king, however, sent out the famous engineer Bautista Antonelli, who fortified Cartagena, Portobelo, Nombre de Dios, Panamá, Santo Domingo, San Juan de Ulúa, the Bay of

Fonseca, and Puerto Caballo and drew up plans for the historic Morro Castles in both Puerto Rico and Havana, where the remains still stand. In 1588 (March 16) Philip named the highly skilled Alexandre Italiano to fortify Brazil, and the king followed explicitly the plans of Pedro Sarmiento de Gamboa for artillery installations on the winding coastline of the Straits of Magellan. His great care in selecting viceroys, his solicitous laws protecting the Indians, his constant preoccupation with the economy of America are all highminded acts that should be enough to save Philip from the unjust reproaches of posterity.

But there is something more essential in the policy of Philip II as ruler of a great nation, which made an unmistakable imprint upon Spanish history. Philip II incarnated and represented the Catholic spirit of the Spanish people; and the defense of Catholicism became the most important motive for his actions. For this reason Spanish troops fought in Flanders, and for this reason he acted against the Huguenots. In order that France would not be ruled by a heretic, he himself pressed his pretensions to the French throne; and in his bitter contest with England, he desired to avenge the death of the Martyr Queen and to come to the aid of English Catholics.

Closely allied with his deep religious feeling and strong religious convictions was another very human compulsion. Philip II acted always as a Spaniard: with dignity. His deeds were impregnated with an *hidalgo* ethic based on honor, the precious knightly legacy of the Middle Ages, which has been and is the theme of Spanish history. What a contrast to the predatory nations, without morals or scruples, whose basis for expansion has been piracy, depredation, and iniquitous despoliation!

Character and Imperial Policy

RAFAEL ALTAMIRA Y CREVEA

Rafael Altamira y Crevea (1866–1951) ranks as one of Spain's outstanding historians. Born in Alicante, he studied law at the University of Valencia and the University of Madrid. After completing his formal education, he first turned his attention to newspaper work but left this profession to become Professor of the History of Spanish Law at the University of Oviedo. Then, in 1914, he moved to the University of Madrid to take the Chair of the Civil and Political Institutions of America. After World War I he helped lay plans for the Permanent Court of International Justice for the League of Nations. Altamira was one of the Spanish "Generation of '98," that group of intellectuals eager to revitalize and reform Spain. For Altamira history must play a highly significant role in any Spanish revival, for it would show, he believed, that Spaniards were like, not different from, other men. His own historical writing, therefore, especially his four-volume *Historia de España y de la civilización española* was devoted to attacking or correcting the distortions and legends concerning Spain and Spanish history. He did not, however, lose his objectivity in patriotic panegyrics. For the most part he adhered to the evidence, even if it did not fit his pro-Spanish bias.

A sick man, worn out in mind and body by the continuous conflicts and unremitting anxieties that gave him no respite during the thirty-nine years of his reign, Charles I in 1556 abdicated the Crown of Spain in favor of his son Philip II. He also adjudged to Philip the Kingdom of Naples, the Duchy of Milan (proceeding from possessions of the German Empire in Italy), Flanders (northern and southern) with the Franche-Comté (an ancient province of France), and Luxembourg: the domains, that is to say, pertaining to the House of Burgundy. This last concession, together with the marriage that Charles himself negotiated between his son Philip and Mary Tudor, future Queen of England (daughter of Henry VIII and Katharine of Aragon, and granddaughter therefore of Ferdinand and Isabella), were the two great culminating mistakes — from the point of view of Spain's national interests — committed by Charles I. Philip would have preferred to inherit, in addition to the Crown of Spain, the Imperial dominions in Italy, which possessed a long Spanish tradition, unlike the domains of the House of Burgundy which bore no relation whatever to the interests of the Spanish Crown. He had to resign himself, nevertheless, to the decision of his father, whose mind was also set on the matrimonial alliance with the English royal family.

The first of these errors resulted in perpetuating and increasing the burden that had weighed on Spain ever since Philip the Fair's death had brought about incorporation into the kingdom of the States pertaining to the Houses of Burgundy and Austria. Not only were parts of these States coveted by the French Kings, but religious difficulties were soon to kindle in them a war that, logically enough, sparked the national sentiment of independence in those countries. The second error soon brought about another conflict, also religious in

From Rafael Altamira y Crevea, *A History of Spain from the Beginnings to the Present Day,* trans. by Muna Lee (New York, 1958), pp. 365–377, 383–384, and 387–389. Reprinted by permission of D. Van Nostrand Company, Inc.

origin, because of the fact that Mary Tudor, a Catholic, persecuted the Protestants; a proceeding on her part disapproved by her husband Philip II, who thereupon recommended a conciliatory attitude of preaching and persuasion toward the English Protestants. In Flanders this latter tactic was soon replaced by violence, as we shall see when we turn our attention to that country.

But Charles I's imperialist ambitions made his point of view in these matters different from Philip's. Charles' imperialism, which was like that of most European monarchs of his time, is understandable according to the political ideology of the period; but that fact is neither palliation nor excuse for the consequences to Spain's future internal development which were consequent on his actions.

The succession to the Crown as Emperor, Charles decided in favor of his brother Ferdinand, who in March, 1558, was recognized as Emperor of Germany by the Prince Electors meeting in the Diet of Frankfort. Six months later Charles I of Spain and V of Germany died at the Monastery of Yuste in Estremadura, to which he had retired in search of rest for body and mind.

From the Spanish national point of view, the most important of the Kings of the House of Austria, and the most Spanish, was Philip II. The volume and influence of his action in government were as great in the sixteenth century as had been those of Ferdinand and Isabella in the fifteenth. But the principal problems that Philip II had to confront differed from those solved by the Catholic Kings (and from those of Isabella particularly) by being for the most part problems that were essentially foreign to Spain and that arose from relations good or bad with other countries. Open attacks and overt threats by monarchs hostile to the House of Austria and to its power in Europe contributed not a little to this state of things. More than once, in order to preserve the independence and defend the national interests of Spain, Philip II found

it necessary to fight enemies banded together. But the fact also had weight that Philip II, although he did not inherit the Empire, continued to strive resolutely for the objectives characteristically imperial, which, to his thinking, had been virtually transmitted to him along with the Spanish Crown. The difference between his imperialist criterion and that of Charles II was that Charles looked on the Empire from the standpoint of an Austrian and a Hapsburg, while Philip II's point of view was that of a Catholic, for whom the supreme necessity was to save the world (not Spain alone) from the heresy triumphant in northern and part of central Europe. This perhaps was Philip's chief political error with respect to Spanish interests; notwithstanding the general humane sentiment of his purpose, within the ideology of the era. It is open to question, however, whether (apart from reasons of religion and of supporting the Imperial family) Philip II was capable of understanding wherein lay the interests of that realm which he had inherited through his father from Isabella of Castile and Ferdinand of Aragon. The only aspects of that national interest which Philip seems properly to have understood in their every phase were Spanish cultural life and the economic necessity of increasing land use in Spain through improving the physiographical environment. Philip's efforts to harmonize what he regarded as his international obligations with the duties of a Spanish King at that period, constituted both his most serious political error and his major inner tragedy.

Philip had been carefully educated to rule by his father, Charles I, and by various persons of culture and experience who surrounded him in his youth. With the purpose of completing that education and of becoming acquainted at first hand with the European countries pertaining to his Empire, Charles had had Philip visit Italy, Flanders, and Germany. Not long afterward, in consequence of his marriage to

Mary Tudor, Philip resided for some time in England.

With all this, he became personally acquainted with the men and the problems that were then stirring Europe, and he acquired very markedly a high sense of his own responsibility as ruler, within the absolutist concept. That sense of responsibility was brought to bear in two ways characteristic of Philip II's method of government: one was his direct personal intervention in all administrative questions; the other, his tenacious defense of the interests of the monarchy against all its enemies, including the Pope when the latter mixed in matters affecting the dominions of the Spanish Crown or its sovereignty.

Philip's personal and direct intervention, symptomatic of his independence of character and zeal for his functions as king, was evidenced in that he never delegated the solution of problems to anyone else, not even to those in whom he had most complete confidence — his secretaries — but studied and solved them himself. That method of procedure, in part deserving of praise, had its disadvantages. By centralizing government down to its last details in himself, he took away initiative from all officials lower in rank than the king, and left them powerless to make decisions even on pressing occasions when there was no time for delay. Moreover, taking into consideration the inevitable slowness of communication in those days, the necessity of awaiting direct instructions from the king resulted often in receiving his orders too late for achieving the desired result. Added to this were Philip's innate vacillations and slowness, which, whatever the psychological explanation, constituted what practically amounted to an inferiority complex on his part when confronted by the dynamic energy demonstrated by his enemies, in particular Queen Elizabeth of England and Catherine de Medici, Queen Mother and Regent of France. The only exception to this bureaucratic technique that Philip employed was the system of legislative autonomies, at times very ample, which he

applied in Spain's American and Oceanic colonies. This was the origin of abundant legislation in code and custom which in practice modified in not a few respects the laws dictated from Spain.

Another of Philip II's characteristics, already referred to in passing, was his sense of juridical responsibility regarding application of and respect for the laws. At first glance it is not easy to understand why that particular monarch had that particular good trait, which is seemingly contradictory to, for example, his dealings with his secretary Antonio Pérez, the punishment he meted out for the uprisings at Saragossa, and similar incidents to be considered in due course. But if we set against these missteps other of Philip's actions and attitudes, such as the respect that he showed for the Aragonese *fuero* in relation to the appointment of the new Viceroy; his refusal to let the vanquished *Moriscos* be expelled; his renunciation of all ownership in a house which he had thought to be his own property, when a woman of the working class disputed his title and convinced him that she had the better claim; his acceptance of the Aragonese import tax *fuero*, invoked with respect to some articles imported by Philip for his own personal use; and many other analogous incidents: all these make one hesitate to say what was Philip's basic characteristic. Was it the underlying impulse that often causes men to sin, repent, and perform good works by way of amends without feeling constrained therefore to sin no more? Or were these apparent contradictions not contradictions in basic doctrine, but rather differences of criteria, arising perhaps from different circumstances of the cases in point regarding, sometimes, observance of the laws and, again, the king's right to inflict punishment? This possible explanation is not rendered inacceptable by exceptions to it such as Acevedo's assassination, which was an act of injustice for which no extenuation can be offered.

Another criterion must be brought to bear, because it was within the political

ethic of the period (to which I shall return), on the inflexible severity with which
Philip II acted in religious matters, in
affairs related to "reasons of State," and in
all things affecting his personal sovereignty;
so that he felt no hesitation in having a
presumed critic poisoned and might have
thrown a fagot with his own hands on the
flames consuming a heretic even though the
heretic had been his son. Philip saw in all
this only just and faithful application of
the law applying in each case. To acts of
this category belongs also his conduct with
regard to the religious question in Flanders
and the Netherlands; an expression of
which was his instructions to successive
Governors there, warning them that they
could yield on some points but never on
any that was "in detriment to our Holy
Catholic Faith, because I shall never consent to the slightest weakening in this, not
even though these dominions be lost
thereby."

The resolute determination to crush
Protestantism which characterized Philip
II led him to come to an understanding
with the Catholic parties in France, England, Ireland, and Scotland, and to aid
them in their struggle against adherents of
the Reformation in their respective countries. Because of this he had to keep up
warfare more or less related to the politi-
cally motivated wars to which we have
referred previously and which influenced
these latter greatly.

So it was in the Netherlands, which
Philip had inherited from the House of
Burgundy. These domains held little interest for him. He entrusted their government first to his natural sister, Margaret,
Duchess of Parma, and a council composed of William, Prince of Orange and
Count of Nassau, known as William the
Silent; Counts Egmont and Horn; and
other eminent personages of the country.
In addition to this Council, Philip placed
at Margaret's side as Prime Minister Cardinal Granvelle, a learned man but stiff-
necked and hardheaded. This appointment
was very unwelcome to the Flemings and

the Dutch, because Granvelle, a native of
the Franche-Comté, was a foreigner. Bad
feeling was engendered by the changes
which Philip introduced in the two bishop-
rics and which were regarded as fore-
runners of the Inquisition, and gave rise
to the deduction that persecution of Calvinists and other Protestants would be
intensified. After several embassies of the
high Flemish nobility demanding government reform, Philip acceded to Granvelle's
dismissal, but he could not bring himself
to slacken his persecution of non-Catholics.
In one of the King's personal letters to his
sister, he told her that he was ready to burn
60,000 or 70,000 persons, if need be, in
order to wipe out heresy in Flanders.

Then commenced the resistance, which
Margaret checked by suspending the trials
of Protestants. Philip himself made some
concessions: suppression of the Inquisition
was among them. One sector of Dutch and
Flemish opinion deemed these concessions
insufficient, and its opposition set off an
insurrection that sacked Catholic churches
in spite of the fact that Lutherans and other
persons of weight in the community opposed such acts of violence. Philip responded to the attack by implanting a system of harsh repression. Accordingly, he
sent the Duke of Alba with instructions
to put down not only the heresy but every
movement favorable to the traditional au-
tonomy of those regions or even merely
representative of opposition to the royal
policy of a strong central government.
Alba carried out these instructions with
utmost severity, even going beyond the
King's order in this respect. The result was
to set in operation simultaneously in the
minds of the Flemish and the Dutch the
two principal mainsprings of action when
peoples rebel against governments: national
freedom and religious freedom. War broke
out, under leadership of William the Silent
and his brother Louis (1568), and Alba
condemned to death Count Egmont and
Count Horn and other personages. With
the situation thus dominated by terrorism,
war flared up again in 1572, and was then

waged by the Low Countries (Holland, Zeeland, Gelderland, Overijssel, Utrecht). It lasted until 1597, and brought in its train many vicissitudes, victories, defeats, and much heroism on both sides. Philip II, disheartened and near to death, ceded the low countries of the North — though retaining Spain's protectorate over them — to Archduke Albert of Austria, to whom he married his daughter the Princess Isabella Clara Eugenia (August, 1597). Philip provided, however, that if their marriage were without issue, in case of the death of either, those States should revert to the Crown of Spain. But he failed of his purpose, because later on these lands were again to burden Spain's strength, and there was renewal of the strife which terminated only with Dutch independence.

The only satisfaction that remained to Philip II was that of seeing that the southern regions of Flanders (corresponding in part to what is now Belgium) remained Catholic for the most part. As regards the religious struggles in France, Philip also found relative compensation in the fact that King Henri IV (1594–1610), although a Protestant in religion, had to be converted to Catholicism in order to be able to control the political situation and conquer the united forces of the King of Spain and of the French Catholics.

The wars with England had an unhappy ending for Spain. Philip planned the invasion of the British Isles so that he could fight on their own ground the English Protestants and Elizabeth their Queen, who consistently favored the rebellious Dutch and Philip's Portuguese enemies, and who were also attacking his possessions in the West Indies. For the invasion he outfitted a large fleet which he called the *Armada Invencible* — the Invincible Armada; but it was as a matter of fact badly equipped, much of its personnel was incompetent, and its commander, the Duke of Medina Sidonia, lacked naval experience. The fleet was shattered by storm and then overcome by English vessels (swifter and better armed than the Spanish ships), notwith-standing the heroism of many Spanish captains (1588). Although soon after this the Spanish obtained several victories over the English, they could not carry out their purpose of invasion, and the destruction of the Invincible Armada not only struck a heavy blow at Spanish morale, but gave rise abroad (especially in England) to a conviction that Spain lacked ability in naval warfare. As for Philip II, he received news of the disaster serenely, and expressed his reaction to it by saying (and therewith touching upon only part of the facts), "I did not send my ships to fight the tempest."

Another most lamentable episode — this time within the family circle — troubled the current of the King's life. It had to do with his first-born son, Prince Don Carlos. The facts relating to this tragic incident have been not only often exaggerated, but sometimes supplanted by stories utterly without historical proof, or by facile hypotheses maliciously accepted as truth. In the first place, Philip II's affection for his children, as revealed by his letters, would never authorize *a priori* supposition of any spontaneous and unjustified severity on his part toward Prince Carlos.

What can be stated, on the basis of actual testimony of extant authentic documents, is, in the first place, that Don Carlos' mind was unbalanced and that his mental instability increased progressively as he grew older. It happened therefore that he frequently committed insensate actions of which he himself was first to suffer the consequences, and which not seldom affected his father and persons of high standing at Court. It is not straining a point to assume that this mental unbalance was at the root of his attempt to flee and join the Dutch, who were rebelling against the rule of the King of Spain. Whatever the circumstantial justification there might be for his wanting to do such a thing, from the standpoint of personal judgments by men today, who take into consideration certain aspirations and acts that do not look the same from every point of view, the indubitable certainty is that

that design of the Prince's was totally irreconcilable from the standpoint of the Spanish State with his condition as Prince and heir presumptive to the Spanish throne. In no Court of the world, nor in any reigning family, would such an attitude as his have been tolerated in that epoch; and if it had been evidenced, harsh repressive measures would have been taken. Such was Philip II's procedure in ordering that the Prince be taken into custody and kept in seclusion in rooms of the Royal Palace.

Although the document in which the King officially communicated this news to various groups and corporations (among them, the Municipal Council of Madrid) does not state in so many words the reason for his decision, it says with utmost clarity, and over and over again — in different forms but always with the same meaning — that there were "very just causes and considerations which concern the service of God and the public welfare of these Kingdoms" and were "of just foundation and purpose."

Six months later the Prince died at the Palace in consequence of the imprudences and eccentricities that his illness and his own violent nature impelled him to commit. We know of no evidence affording any basis for a supposition that either his father the King or the Inquisition had a hand in his death.

Philip II also gave great encouragement to cultural developments, his interest finding expression not only in the support given the universities and other instruments of study and research, but also in the development of libraries and in the aid amply granted to workers in the fields of the plastic arts, music, and the sciences. Among the educational foundations established by Philip II were the Academy of Sciences, which functioned in the Royal Palace itself with sessions attended by nobles and officers of the armed services; the Academy of Mathematics, the first director of which was the architect-engineer Herrera, designer of the Escorial, and in which were studied hydraulics, architecture, cosmography, navigation, artillery, and the construction of forts and city walls; the specialized library of this latter Academy for which books were procured from all over Europe, and its great collection of machines and instruments for use in experiments; the Botanical Garden at Aranjeuz; the magnificent Library of the Escorial; the Spanish Archives at Rome and at Simancas; the scientific expedition to the Americas led by Dr. Francisco Hernández, which was fitted out with everything to be had in the way of equipment and facilities for such an undertaking and which resulted in great botanical and pharmaceutical discoveries; the preservation and classification of the botanical collections coming from the New World, a task that the King confided to the eminent naturalist Antonio Nardo; et cetera. The scientific importance of the Academies mentioned was far-reaching, one of the many reasons for this being the fact that they very usefully supplemented the teaching of the Universities, which had come to be deficient in scientific branches. Thus, while such university courses were declining, especially in the disciplines being renovated by the Renaissance, the Academies kept more in step with European progress. A Spanish historian commenting upon them opines that the closing later on of some of the Academies was the principal cause of the decadence of certain studies in seventeenth-century Spain. About this same time (1645), the English created their Royal Society, the leading scientific association in Great Britain.

Philip II was also originator of the project for establishing a monopoly of the publication of religious books, for which purpose he obtained a license from the Pope and gave large subsidies to several presses. The most important of these was the Plantín Press, where the erudite Spaniard Arias Montano supervised printing of the Polyglot Bible with the original text and its translations into several languages printed in parallel columns for purposes of comparison, a monumental edition unique except for the Complutensian Polyglot Bible (published in Spain in 1522), from which it is quite distinct. The building where the Plantín Press was installed may still be visited at Antwerp.

To Philip II's time belong some of the most illustrious Spanish scientists, artists, and men-of-letters, who, lending lustre to what has been called the Age of Gold and famous in their own time, are not all forgotten, since much of their work is still a living force today.

The reigns of Charles I and Philip II coincided also with the great period of the Spanish universities, of which Salamanca was the most famous.

It is an interesting fact that the multiplicity of heterogeneous matters demanding attention and action by the King and by public officials made necessary the making of many laws and the publication of a new code of Spanish internal law. That Code, repeatedly requested by the Cortes in petitions concerned with the confusion among the Castilian Crown's ancient juridical sources, which confusion had been augmented since the reign of the Catholic Kings by the new legislation, was promulgated in 1567 under the title *Nueva Recopilación,* or New Code. Many efforts were made, as we shall see, to publish colonial legislation separately.

SUGGESTIONS FOR FURTHER READING

Ruling for almost half a century over the greatest empire the world had ever known, Philip II has evoked an immense quantity of historical literature. This list in no way pretends to be exhaustive but is merely a sampling of the many works on the Prudent King. For an evaluation of research on the reign of Philip II and his accomplishments, see Carl Georg Bratli, *Philippe II, roi d'Espagne: étude sur sa vie et son caractère* (Paris, 1912), particularly pp. 17–55 and 239–284 for an extensive bibliography and interpretation of the literature on Philip. Roger B. Merriman's *Philip the Prudent*, Vol. IV of *The Rise of the Spanish Empire* (New York, 1934) presents a full discussion of source materials and other works on the Spanish monarch, pp. 69–77, 157–160, 320–321, 403–406, and 669–670. Rafael Altamira y Crevea, *Ensayo sobre Felipe II: hombre de estado: su psicología general y su individualidad humana* (Mexico, D. F., 1950) contains an extensive but repetitious and often inaccurate bibliography on all aspects of Philip's reign, pp. 289–395. R. Ballester y Castell, *Las fuentes narrativas de la historia de España durante la edad moderna (1407–1808)* (Valladolid, 1927), pt. 3, pp. 147–204, presents a perceptive discussion of Philip's biographers. Several recent historiographical essays can be used as supplements to the studies listed above. Léon E. Halkin, "La physionomie morale de Philippe II, d'après ses derniers biographes," *Revue historique* CLXXIX (1937), 355–367. Halkin's article was redrafted into a broader, less technical essay and published in his *Initiation à la critique historique* (2nd rev. ed. Paris: 1953), pp. 99–119, which is reprinted in English translation in this present group of selections; see pp. 61–67. Also of interest to the reader are Richard Konetzke, "Zur Biographie Philipps II von Spanien," *Historische Zeitschrift* CLXIV (1941), 316–331; and H. Lapeyre, "Autour de Philippe II," *Bulletin hispanique* LIX (1957), 152–175. The latter article assesses the work of eight of Philip's latest biographers.

There are several excellent general histories of Spain in English. Perhaps the best is Rafael Altamira y Crevea, *A History of Spain from the Beginnings to the Present Day*, trans. Muna Lee (New York, 1949). Three other concise, general histories are Louis Bertrand and Sir Charles Petrie, *The History of Spain* (London, 1952); Harold Livermore, *A History of Spain* (London, 1958); and Salvador de Madariaga, *Spain: A Modern History* (New York, 1958), the latter bearing mostly on the nineteenth and twentieth centuries. General accounts in English more specifically oriented to the period of Philip II are R. Trevor Davies, *The Golden Century of Spain, 1501–1621* (London, 1937) and Martin A. S. Hume, *Spain: Its Greatness and Decay, 1479–1788* (Cambridge, 1925). A classic general account is Antonio Ballesteros y Beretta, *Historia de España y su influencia en la historia universal,* 9 vols. (Barcelona, 1917–1941), vol. IV, pts. 1 and 2. A more recent work on the period is P. Luis Fernández and Fernández de Retana, *España en tiempo de Felipe II, (1556–1598)* (Madrid, 1958). Beautifully illustrated and remarkably balanced in its account, this was published in two parts as vol. XIX in the monumental *Historia de España,* edited by Ramón Menéndez Pidal. Despite their pro-Spanish bias, Ballesteros, Altamira, Fernández, and de Retana represent a high standard of historical scholarship. Two standard works in French are Henri Hauser, *La prépondérance espagnole (1559–1660)* (Paris, 1934), vol. IX in the *Peuples et civilisations* series; and J. H. Mariéjol, "Le Réforme et la Ligue — L'Édit de Nantes (1559–1598)" in *Histoire* de France depuis les origines jusqu'à la révolution, ed. Ernest Lavisse (Paris, 1911), vol. VI, pt. 1.

There are many published documents bearing on Philip's life and reign. Perhaps the individual who has done the most to help bring Philip into a clearer historical perspective is Louis P. Gachard, the Belgian bibliophile and historian. His *Lettres de Philippe II à ses filles, les infantes Isabelle et Catherine écrites pendant son voyage en Portugal (1581–1583)* (Paris, 1884) show Philip to be a loving, understanding father devoted to his children. The *Relations des ambassadeurs Vénétiens sur Charles Quint et Philippe II* (Brussels, 1855) were reports of Venetian ambassadors in Spain used in manuscript by Ranke to put Philip in a more favorable light. See also Eugenio Albèri, ed. *Relazioni degli ambasciatori Veneti durante il secolo decimosesto*, serie I, vols. ii, iii, v, and vi (Florence, 1839–1862). Other documents edited by Gachard are *Correspondance de Philippe II sur les affaires des Pays-Bas (1558–77)* (Brussels, 1848–1879), 5 vols.; *Particularités inédites sur les derniers moments de Philippe II* (Brussels, 1848); and *Correspondance d'Alexandre Farnèse avec Philippe II pour les années 1578, 1579* (Brussels, 1853).

A useful collection of Spanish documents is the *Colección de documentos inéditos para la historia de España* (Madrid, 1842–1895), 112 vols. These volumes contain a potpourri of material on Philip's reign and the full text of many documents merely summarized in another significant collection, Martin A. S. Hume, ed. *Calendar of State Papers, Spanish: 1558–1603* (London, 1892–99), 4 vols. The *Collection de documents inédits sur l'histoire de France*, première série, histoire politique, includes a series of volumes edited by Charles Weiss, *Papiers d'état de Cardinal de Granvelle* (Paris, 1841–1852), 9 vols. Particularly revealing is vol. III, pp. 267–319, which contains the instructions of Charles I to his son Philip. On the period of the formation of the Armada, see A.

Mousset, ed., *Dépêches diplomatiques de M. de Longlée, Résident de France en Espagne (1582–1590)* (Paris, 1912) and C. Fernández Duro, *La armada invencible* (Madrid, 1884–85), 2 vols. On Philip's relations with the papacy see Ricardo de Hinojosa, ed., *Los despachos de la diplomacia pontificia en España* (Madrid, 1896) and L. Serrano Sanz, ed., *Correspondencia diplomática entre España y la Santa Sede durante el pontificado de Pio V* (Madrid, 1914), 4 vols. Two other collections are A. Teulet, ed., *Relations politiques de la France et de l'Espagne avec l'Écosse* (Paris, 1862) and F. S. Thessier, ed., *Correspondance de Marguerite d'Autriche avec Philippe II* (Utrecht, 1925).

Accounts written during or soon after the reign of Philip II may prove particularly useful to the serious student. Perhaps the best known is the monumental four-volume work of Luis Cabrera de Córdoba, *Felipe Segundo, Rey de España* (Madrid, 1876) 4 vols. The first part of his work, on Philip to 1583, first appeared in 1619, but the entire work was not published until 1876–77. An important royal functionary, Cabrera took copious notes while the king was still alive in preparation for his life of Philip. Cabrera, however, was something of a plagiarist and borrowed a great deal of material from another significant contemporary chronicler, Antonio de Herrera y Tordesillas, *Historia general del mundo del tiempo del rey Felipe II, el prudente* (Madrid, 1601–1612), 3 vols. Baltasar Porreños was a contemporary of both Cabrera and Herrera. His eulogistic *Dichos y hechos del rey Felipe Segundo* (Cuenca, 1621), remained the standard Spanish work on Philip for over two centuries. Two other useful contemporary accounts are Juan Gines de Sepúlveda, *De rebus gestis Philippe II* in *Obras Completas*, vol. III (Madrid, 1780) on the early life of the Prudent King; and José de Sigüenza (1544–1606), *Historia del monasterio del Escorial* (Madrid, 1927). Sigüenza's account is still the basic work on the subject with which it deals.

Contemporary accounts published outside Spain were bitter attacks on Philip II. William the Silent's *Apologia of 1580,* (London, 1581) from which we have included a selection (see pp. 8–10) was so vitriolic that it has been labeled a "psychological document." It did, however, serve useful political ends. Condemning Philip as an incestual religious fanatic, treacherous and murderous, William's view became exceedingly popular in most of western Europe, especially in England, where the *Apologia* was immediately translated and published.

Antonio Pérez, in his *Relaciones de Antonio Pérez* (Paris, 1594) and in numerous other editions, did much to give credence to William's portrait of the Spanish monarch. All of the details of the Pérez story are not clear, but he became Philip's secretary and principal adviser in 1573 after the death of the Duke of Eboli. In 1578, Philip and Pérez plotted the murder of Juan de Escovedo, secretary to Don John of Austria, hero of Lepanto. Suddenly, however, because of a change in circumstances, the murder became unnecessary. Pérez carried out the plot anyway. When gossip in Madrid linked Pérez and the Princess of Eboli, widow of Pérez's predecessor, to Escovedo's murder, it became embarrassing for the King, who finally seized them both. Unlike the Princess of Eboli, who died in prison, Pérez was put under house arrest and later released, but in 1584 was finally convicted for tampering with state papers. Four years later in 1588 he was put on trial for Escovedo's murder on the basis of a confession wrenched from him by means of judicial torture. Ultimately, however, he escaped to Aragon, where he enjoyed immunity from arrest under an old Aragonese privilege (*manifestación*). Philip tried hard to extradite Pérez, but failed. Pérez, in turn, was successful in linking his own fate to traditional Aragonese rights, and riots broke out. These gave Philip II the excuse he needed to invade Aragon and seize Pérez, but the slippery secretary managed to escape to France in 1591. Wandering

about both France and England and enjoying favors of the royal courts in both countries, he wrote a violent exposé of the court of Philip II. Merriman points out that the *Relaciones* were published four times in Paris and twice in Geneva before the end of the seventeenth century, but were not published in Spain until 1849. Pérez's influence may be seen very clearly in the two-volume biography written by Gregorio Leti, *Vita del catolico ré Filippo II* (Cologne, 1679), 2vols. in one, a violent anti-Philip polemic.

Another significant contemporary account critical of Philip was written by Jean Auguste de Thou (1559–1617), *Jano Augusti Thuani historiarum sui temporis* (London, 1733), 7 vols. Published initially between 1604 and 1620, De Thou's work was influenced by both Pérez and De Thou's Huguenot beliefs. In Paris during the Massacre of the Eve of Saint Bartholomew's Day, he was so horrified and sickened by what he saw that he ultimately became a champion of religious tolerance. In De Thou's view, Philip II was a bigoted zealot, who perpetrated evil in the name of religion.

For biographies other than those extracted for this study, the reader may find the following useful. Henri Forneron, *Histoire de Philippe II* (Paris, 1881–1882), 4 vols., traces Philip's reign in great detail but should be employed with caution because of the carelessness with which Forneron cites his sources. Solid late nineteenth-century works are Reinhold Baumstark, *Philipp II. König von Spanien* (Freiburg, 1875); Martin Philippson, "König Philipp von Spanien," in *Der neue Plutarch,* III (1876), 1–116; and Jean H. Mariéjol, *Philip II, the First Modern King* (New York, 1933), published in England under the title *The Master of the Armada: The Life and Reign of Philip II,* trans. by W. B. Wells (London, 1933). Mariéjol's work is an expansion of an early essay on Philip which appeared as "L'Oeuvre de Philippe II," from vol. V of Lavisse and Rambaud, *Histoire générale du IVe siècle à nos jours*

(Paris, 1896), 49–107. Martin A. S. Hume's *Philip II of Spain* (London, 1899) presents a late-Victorian Englishman's view of Philip's reign, one which is remarkably fair and dispassionate. In the twentieth century there has appeared a school of Philippine apologists. One of the better-known works of this school is José Fernández Montana's *Felipe II el Prudente y su política* (Madrid, 1914), which brings together the findings of his earlier books: *Nueva luz y juicio verdadero sobre Felipe II* (Madrid, 1891) and *Mas luz de verdad histórica sobre Felipe II el prudente* (Madrid, 1892). Books by other members of this school are Jean Cassou's *La vie de Philippe II* (Paris, 1929); Louis Pfandl, *Philippe II: Une époque, un homme, un roi* (Paris, 1942), translated from the German work *Philipp II. Gemälde eines Lebens und einer Zeit* (Munich, 1938); David Loth, *Philip II of Spain* (London and New York, 1932); Reinhold Schneider, *Philipp der Zweite, oder Religion und Macht* (Leipzig, 1931); and William T. Walsh, *Philip II* (London, 1937). Many passages from Walsh are included in C. J. Cadoux, *Philip of Spain and the Netherlands: An Essay on Moral Judgments in History* (London, 1947); see particularly pp. 31–36.

For studies on Philip's psychological make-up see the works by Fidel Pérez Minguez, *Psicología de Felipe II* (Madrid, 1925) and Rafael Altamira y Crevea, *Ensayo sobre Felipe II: hombre de estado: su psicología general y su individualidad humana* (Mexico, D. F., 1950).

There are many monographs and specialized studies on various aspects of the age of Philip II. This list is only representative and is drawn up to give the student a summary guide to the significant works in the field.

The Spanish Empire: Two recen works are indispensable to the study of Philip II's vast empire. First, Fernand Braudel, *La Méditerranée et le monde méditerranéen à l'époque de Philippe II* (Paris, 1949) represents an important advance in historiog-raphy in which the historian attempts to combine his own methods with those of the geographer and the sociologist. The implications of Braudel's work are spelled out in the essay by Edward R. Tannenbaum, "French Scholarship in Modern European History: New Developments since 1945," *Journal of Modern History*, XXIX (September, 1947), 246–252. A second important work on the Empire is Bohdan Chudoba, *Spain and the Empire, 1519–1643* (Chicago, 1952), which is a study of the Hapsburgs' imperial problems from the accession of Charles V to the Battle of Rocroi. Chudoba is particularly acute in his analysis of the relationships between the Hapsburgs in Vienna and those in Madrid. His portrait of Philip II, pp. 79–100, is a balanced one incorporating the most recent scholarship. Other studies on the Empire are Roger B. Merriman's sober and well-balanced *Rise of the Spanish Empire*, vol. IV: *Philip the Prudent* (New York, 1934) and the highly factual account of Eduardo Ibarra y Rodríguez, *España bajo los Austrias* (Barcelona, 1955).

More specialized studies on the Empire may be found in H. G. Koenigsberger, *The Government of Sicily under Philip II of Spain* (London, 1959), which shows Philip's great concern for his possessions in Southern Italy and his shrewdness as an imperial administrator. Lucien Febvre's perceptive and exhaustively researched doctoral thesis presents an important study of the early years of Philip's reign, *Philippe II et la Franche-Comté: La crise de 1569. Étude d'histoire politique, religieuse, et sociale* (Paris, 1911). See also M. Constance, "Spanish Rule in the Netherlands under Philip II," *Catholic Historical Review*, VIII (1928), 365–422; P. O. de Törne, *Don Juan d'Autriche et les projets de conquête de l'Angleterre. Étude historique sur dix années du XVIe siècle, 1568–1578* (Helsinki, 1915–1928), 2 vols.; P. O. de Törne, "Philippe II et Henri de Guise. Le début de leurs relations (1578)," *Revue historique*, CLXVIII (1931), 323–335. For a more extensive account of

Franco-Spanish relations see Joseph de Croze, *Les Guises, les Valois, et Philippe II* (Paris, 1866). Still quite useful is J. W. Thompson, *The Wars of Religion in France, 1559–1576: The Huguenots, Catherine de Medici and Philip II* (Chicago, 1909). For a more modern interpretation of the beginnings of the religious war in France, see Robert M. Kingdon, *Geneva and the Coming of the War of Religion in France, 1555–1563* (Geneva, 1956). For a balanced account of the Dutch revolt read Pieter Geyl, *The Revolt of the Netherlands (1555–1609)*, (London, 1958). Geyl, though stigmatizing Philip as a "short-sighted, unbending and detested" ruler in the Low Countries, recognized the fact that Philip simply followed policies already laid down by his father, Charles V. For a view of Spanish policy vis-à-vis England, see Garrett Mattingly's brilliant sketch of *Renaissance Diplomacy* (Boston, 1955), which began as a full-length study of Anglo-Spanish relations in the early modern period. Portuguese affairs are explained in J. M. Rubio, *Felipe II y Portugal* (Madrid, 1929). The background to Philip II's claims to Portugal may be found in a recent book by Edward Bovill, *The Battle of Alcázar: An Account of the Defeat of Dom Sebastian of Portugal at El sar el Kebir* (London, 1952).

Philip II and the Church: An excellent introduction to this subject can be found in J. Lynch, "Philip II and the Papacy," *Transactions of the Royal Historical Society*, 5th Series, II (1961), 23–42. An older but reliable account is Martin Philippson, "Felipe II y el Pontificado," *Estudios sobre Felipe II*, ed. R. de Hinojosa (Madrid, 1887), pp. 91–160. Recent and useful is M. Boyd, *Cardinal Quiroga, Inquisitor General of Spain* (Dubuque, 1954). For the Inquisition as a general problem, see the monumental work of Henry Charles Lea, *A History of the Inquisition in Spain* (New York and London, 1906–1907), 4 vols. A favorable picture of the Inquisition is presented by Miguel de la Pinta Llorente in *La Inquisición española* (Madrid, 1948). A balanced account of the Inquisition may

be found in Salvador Fornieles, *La España del siglo XVI: Felipe II y la Inquisición* (Buenos Aires, 1951). For relations of church and state read F. de los Rios, *Religión y estado en la España del siglo XVI* (Madrid, 1928). For a study of Spanish ecclesiastical politics in the Low Countries see Alexander J. Namèche, *Le règne de Philippe II et la lutte religieuse dans les Pays-Bas au XVIe siècle* (Louvain, 1885–1887), 2 vols.; also see B. de Meester, *Le Saint Siège et les troubles des Pays-Bas, 1566–1579* (Louvain, 1934).

Military and Naval History: A standard introduction to military history of the epoch can be found in Sir Charles Oman's *A History of the Art of War in the Sixteenth Century* (London and New York, 1937), pp. 51–62, 254–282, and 506–525. See also Michael Roberts, *The Military Revolution, 1560–1660* (Belfast, [1956]). One of the finest pieces of recent historical investigation in the field of military history is Léon van der Essen's *Alexandre Farnèse, prince de Parme, gouverneur général des Pays-Bas (1545–1592)* (Brussels, 1933–1937), 5 vols. For a study of Lepanto see Sir William Stirling-Maxwell, *Don John of Austria* (London, 1883), 2 vols. For studies of the Armada, Garrett Mattingly's *The Armada* (London and Boston, 1959) supplies the European background in a masterly way. Michael Lewis's *The Spanish Armada* (London, 1960) presents a careful, technical view. Also useful is I. Bauer Landauer, *Consideraciones sobre la política naval de España en el siglo XVI* (Madrid, 1926).

Economic History: Of greatest importance to the student interested in sixteenth-century Spain is the work of Earl J. Hamilton. His *American Treasure and the Price Revolution in Spain, 1501–1650* (Cambridge, 1934) began a new era in the study of Spanish and European economic history. Many of Hamilton's essays are collected and translated into Spanish in *El florecimiento del capitalismo y otros ensayos de historia económica* (Madrid, 1948). For a stimulating critique of Hamilton's position, read David Felix, "Profit Inflation and

Industrial Growth. . . ," *Quarterly Journal of Economics,* LXX (1956), 441–463. Also of interest because of their reassessment of Hamilton's works are John Elliott, "The Decline of Spain," *Past and Present,* no. 20 (1961), 52–75 and Pierre Vilar, "The Problems of the Formation of Capitalism," *Past and Present,* no. 10 (1956), 15–38. Now somewhat outdated but still a helpful guide is H. Berindoague, *Le mercantilisme en Espagne* (Paris, 1929). See also A. Girard, *Le commerce français à Seville et Cadiz au temps des Habsbourgs: Contribution à l'étude du commerce étranger en Espagne aux XVIe et XVIIe siècles* (Paris, 1932) and C. H. Haring, *Trade and Navigation between Spain and the Indies in the Time of the Hapsburgs* (Cambridge, Mass., 1918). The recent work by H. and P. Chaunu is monumental, *Seville et l'Atlantique (1504–1650)* (Paris, 1955–1959), 8 vols. For the latest review of the entire period, see Ladislas Reitzer, "Some Observations on Castilian Commerce and Finance in the Sixteenth Century," *Journal of Modern History,* XXXII (September, 1960), 213–223.

Institutional Studies: An excellent introduction to the conciliar government developed by Philip can be found in J. M. Batista i Roca's "Forward" to H. G. Koenigsberger's *The Government of Sicily under Philip II of Spain* (London, 1951), pp. 9–35. Meticulous in its scholarship is Leon C. Riba y Garcia, *El consejo supremo de Aragón en el reinado de Felipe II* (Valencia, 1914). Also standard is Roger B. Merriman, *The Rise of the Spanish Empire,* Vol. IV, *Philip the Prudent* (New York, 1934), pp. 409–489.

Philip II and the Don Carlos Affair: The mystery surrounding Don Carlos' death has intrigued historians from the sixteenth to the twentieth century, but it was not until the nineteenth century that the facts were weighed objectively. Louis P. Gachard did a great deal to set the record aright in his *Don Carlos et Philippe II* (Paris, 1867). A somewhat more critical view of Philip, adopting the somewhat accusing tone reminiscent of the earlier works of drama-

tists and popularizers is Viktor Bibl, *Der Tod des Don Carlos* (Vienna, 1918). The works on the Don Carlos theme are summarized and evaluated in F. W. C. Lieder, "The Don Carlos Theme," in *Harvard Studies and Notes in Philology and Literature,* XII (1930), 1–73, and in Felix Rachfahl's *Don Carlos, Kritische Untersuchungen* (Freiburg, 1921).

Philip II and Antonio Pérez: The scandal concerning Antonio Pérez described above thrilled both the scandalmongers and the opponents of Spain from the sixteenth century to the present. One of the most notable and most recent biographies of Pérez is G. Marañon, *Antonio Pérez* (Buenos Aires, 1947), 2 vols. Also useful are François A. M. A. Mignet, *Antonio Pérez et Philippe II* (Paris, 1854); the massive work of Pedro José, Marquis de Pidal, *Philippe II, Antonio Pérez et le Royaume d'Aragon* (Paris, 1867), trans. by J. G. Margnabal, 2 vols.; J. A. Froude, "Antonio Pérez: An Unsolved Historical Riddle," in *The Spanish Story of the Armada and Other Essays* (New York, 1905), pp. 90–154; Louis Bertrand, *Philippe II, une ténébreuse affaire* (Paris, 1929), a favorable view, and his *Philippe II contre Antonio Pérez* (Monaco, 1929); and José Fernández Montana in *De cómo Felipe II no mandó matar a Escobedo* (Madrid, 1910).

Philip II and the Escorial: To most Spaniards and the outside world Philip's palace-monastery of San Lorenzo de Escorial in the mountains outside Madrid symbolized the power and the piety of the Spanish monarch. Here in a small apartment overlooking the altar of the church, Philip II labored tirelessly over the affairs of state. In the latter years of his reign he went into almost complete seclusion in the austere baroque edifice, giving rise to the popular legend of Philip as the spider king, weaver of plots and counterplots. For the best descriptions of the Escorial see L. Niño Azcona, *Felipe II y la villa de El Escorial* (Madrid, 1934); Louis Bertrand, *Philippe II à l'Escorial* (Paris, 1928); and Garrett Mattingly, *The Armada* (Boston, 1959), pp. 69–81.